CASH COLLECTION & TRANSMISSION

Brian Coyle

CIB PUBLISHING

FINANCIAL
EDUCATION

CIB Publishing
c/o The Chartered Institute of Bankers
Emmanuel House
4-9 Burgate Lane
Canterbury
Kent
CT1 2XJ
United Kingdom

Telephone: 01227 762600

CIB Publishing publications are published by The Chartered Institute of Bankers, a non-profit making registered educational charity.

Typeset by The Foundry
Printed by WBC Book Manufacturers, Bridgend

ISBN 0-85297-448-5

Contents

1

Introduction

Money has a cost or a value. It has a cost to businesses that don't have it and need to borrow it. It has a value to businesses that can deposit it to earn interest. All companies, large or small, should try to manage their cash to keep interest costs as low as possible, or to achieve high-interest income. Cash management is concerned with using money efficiently and effectively to control interest costs or optimize income.

Companies that either borrow or hold surplus cash have some exposure to interest-rate risk. This is the risk of lower income or higher costs from an adverse change in interest rates. Risk can be hedged (reduced) structurally by avoiding unnecessary cash deficits or surpluses, and cash management should contribute towards this aim.

Where money is held or owed in foreign currency, there is the additional objective of limiting the currency risk. Adverse exchange rate movements could reduce the value of cash held in a foreign currency or increase the cost of currency loans and overdrafts.

A group of companies with several bank accounts around the world and cash flows in different currencies can try to hedge its currency exposures and interest rate exposures by cash management methods, by for example

- matching cash receipts by a subsidiary in one currency with payments in the same currency by another subsidiary
- netting intercompany dealings to minimize transactions with financial institutions
- offsetting the cash surpluses of one division against the borrowing needs of another

- minimizing the group's total external debts.

Organizing exposure management at group level calls for a flexible cash-management system. The group must be able to switch cash from one subsidiary and one bank account to another. Up-to-date and accurate information about the cash position of each subsidiary also is essential.

This book considers three important aspects of cash management: cash collection, banking configurations and electronic banking systems. They concern

- the methods of collecting cash and making payments
- the way in which bank accounts are organized
- the use of electronic systems for making payments and directing money flows.

Cash Collection

Cash payment and cash collection are two aspects of the same money transfer. When a payment is made through the banking system, the payer's account is debited with the amount of the payment and funds are deducted from the account. The account of the payee (recipient) is credited and funds are paid into the account. When the payee's account receives funds that can be spent immediately, the payee is said to have received or obtained *value* for the funds.

The loss of value in the payer's account and the receipt of value in the payee's account do not necessarily occur at the same time or even on the same day. The payer could lose value from his account before the payee obtains value. In the intervening time, the bank of either the paying or payee customer has the benefit to itself of the funds in transfer. For banks, this period is known as the float.

One function of cash management should be to consider how customers make payments. An alternative method of payment might enable the company to receive value more quickly for inward payments or to time the loss of value for outward payments more exactly. Or it might be appropriate to negotiate a quicker processing time with its bank for payments by *existing* methods. In other words, the company should seek methods to reduce the float that represents lost interest revenues.

Float

The float is the amount of cash that has been paid to a company, for which the company has yet to obtain value (cleared funds) at the bank.

Float time is the time between a customer initiating a payment and the company being informed or aware that it has obtained value at the bank.

There are four causes of float time

- transmission delay
- lodgment delay
- clearance delay (bank float time)
- advice delay

Transmission delay is the time between the sending of a payment and its physical receipt by the payee. For electronic transmissions, the delay is until the funds are credited to the account. A check sent by post could take from one day up to several weeks to reach its recipient, depending on the postal service used and the country of dispatch. Payments sent by courier can be received the same day, but at the cost of the courier's fee by the payer or the payee.

Lodgment delay is the time between physical receipt of a payment and banking it. Checks, for example, might not be banked on the day of receipt. They ought to be banked by the next bank working day; even so, a lodgment delay lasting over a weekend would be two or three days. With an inefficient cash-management system, checks could be held for several days before they are banked, perhaps because an envelope containing a check is left unopened, or because of delays in the clerical processing of receipts.

Clearance delay or bank float time is the time between banking money receipts and receiving value for the funds in the bank account.

Advice delay is the time lost between obtaining value for funds received into a bank account and being notified or becoming aware that the funds are available to use.

The speed of cash collection matters because delay costs money. Excessive float can be costly. For a company with an annual turnover of $50 million and paying overdraft interest of 8% per annum, a reduction in float time of just *one day* would produce savings in overdraft interest or higher income from cash deposits of around $11,000 ($50 million ÷ 365 x 8%) because it would improve the average cash balances by $137,000.

The speed with which cash payments are made and the funds cleared in the recipient's bank account depends on

- the method of payment used, and
- whether the payment is domestic or international.

Improving collection times can provide important savings or extra revenue. To understand this aspect of cash management, it helps to know how the banking system operates for cash transmission and clearance of funds.

Clearing

Clearing is the process by which banks exchange checks and other payments, and settle the net differences in payment amounts. At some stage during the clearing process, the accounts of the banks' customers are debited or credited, according to whether they are making or receiving payments. A clearing system for a check written by Alpha and payable to Beta is illustrated in the diagram below.

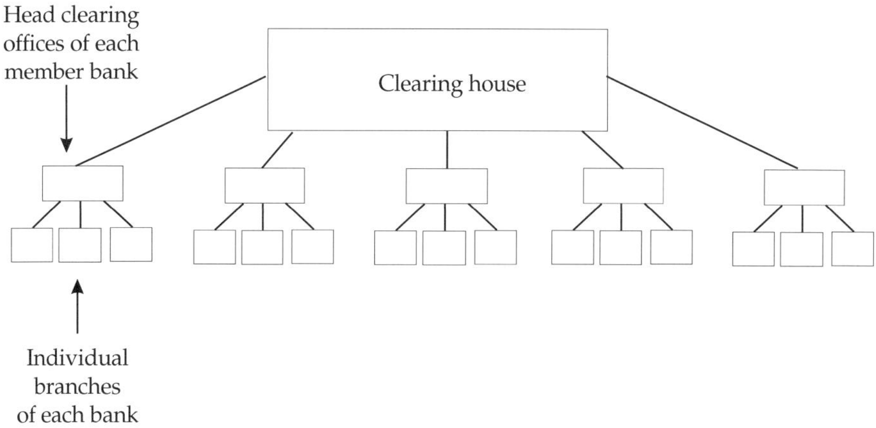

Clearing systems differ between one country and another, and for international payments. The clearing process also will differ according to the method or nature of the payment.

Cash Book, Bank Statement and Cleared Funds

It is easy for a non-banker to be confused by the clearing process. A company at any time can have three differing amounts for its current cash balance.

- A cash book balance
- A bank statement balance
- A cleared funds balance.

There will be a record in the company's accounts of how much cash it has. This is the cash-book balance. When receipts are paid into a bank, the cash book is updated, and the receipts are recorded as additions to its holding of cash.

The bank will update its own accounting records, normally a day or so later, by crediting the customer's account with the receipts paid in. If a bank statement is prepared, this will show the amount of money in the customer's account, as recorded in the bank's accounting records. Some of these funds might not yet have been cleared.

The customer can use money in an account only when payments are finally cleared and he receives value for the funds. A bank statement balance anticipates the cleared balance typically by one or two days.

With payments from an account, updating the bank's accounting records (i.e. updating the bank statement) and the withdrawal of funds from the customer's account occur at the same time.

Banks must be able to provide a customer with information about cleared balances because it is the cleared balance that matters most for day-to-day cash management. This information can be obtained either by telephoning the bank, or by an electronic banking information service.

Example 1
A check for $5,000 is received in the accounts department of Sierra Inc on Monday at 4pm. The receipt is processed before the end of the day and in the accounting records of Sierra, the cash book balance is increased by $5,000.

The check is banked at 2.30pm the following day, Tuesday. It is processed by the local branch that credits Sierra's account on Wednesday with the $5,000.

Sierra receives value for the $5,000 three days after banking it, on the Friday.

Receipt

Example 2
Tango Limited sends a check payment of $6,000 to a supplier by post. The payment is sent out on Monday, when Tango's accounting records are updated, and the cash-book balance is decreased by $6,000.

The supplier receives the payment by post on Tuesday and banks it immediately. In the clearing process, Tango loses the money from its account two days later, on Thursday.

Payment

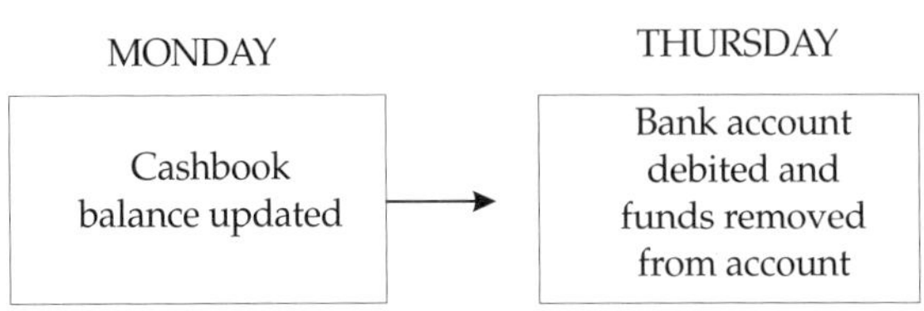

Payment Methods

A variety of payment methods are available, in addition to checks. Clearance time and the clearing process vary according to the payment method.

Notes and Coins

Notes and coins paid into an account do not require clearing. Banks might be reluctant to handle notes and coins in large volumes because they are a non-interest-bearing item, and so have no particular attraction to a bank except as till money. The only exception is cash deposited at the Bank of England that pays interest on amounts held overnight in its bullion operation.

When a company pays notes and coins into its account through its own branch, it might receive value for the funds on the same day, but there could be delay of one day or more. Receiving value for notes and coins paid in through a different branch of the bank could take one or two days. If a different bank is used to pay in notes and coins, value might not be received for three days.

Companies that regularly pay in large quantities of notes and coins should check the value dating delay with their bank.

Banker's Draft

A banker's draft is a check drawn on a bank. A payment by banker's draft is guaranteed (except in the unlikely circumstance of the bank going into liquidation). On request banks will prepare drafts on behalf of a customer. The customer will lose value from his account on the day the draft is written. Recipients of a banker's drafts, on presenting the draft through their own bank, will receive same- day value for the funds.

Credit Cards

Credit card payments can be made by voucher or electronically. Voucher payments are processed in a similar way to checks, through the head office clearing centers of the banks.

Companies banking receipts by credit card voucher (Visa or Mastercard) could receive same-day value for the funds from their bank. However, companies taking credit card payments from customers pay a fee to the credit card company (their bank) of between 1.5% and 5% of the payments received.

Special Presentation of Checks

A situation might occur when a check has been received from a customer but there is serious doubt about the ability of the customer to pay. The payee company could ask its bank to make a *special presentation* of the check. The bank will post the check to the branch at which the paying customer has his account. When the check has been received at the customer's bank (the next morning) the payee's bank can check by telephone to confirm that there are sufficient funds in the account to meet the payment. If there are, the customer loses value from the account that day and this guarantees eventual payment to the payee.

For checks below $100,000, the check will then go through the clearing process, and the payee company will receive good value in two to three days. Larger checks will be substituted by a banker's draft that will be sent direct by post from the customer's bank to the payee company's bank.

A special presentation of a check is a measure that should be taken only in cases of extreme doubt about the customer. A less extreme, and more informal, method of checking is called *advice of fate* whereby the bank is asked to telephone the paying customer's bank and ask if the customer has sufficient funds to meet the payment. Unlike a special presentation of the check, advice of fate does not provide a guarantee of payment, and the check will go through the normal clearing process.

Transfers

Funds can be transferred from one bank account to another on receipt of instructions by the paying bank to make the payment. Instructions can be by telephone (subsequently confirmed in writing), on paper, sent by cable or telex, or electronic processing center.

Summary

Clearance times can vary according to the method of payment. A shorter delay in receiving cleared value does not mean necessarily that the payer loses value earlier, although this often will be the case. Earlier clearance can be obtained if the banks reduce the float time during which they have the use of funds in the clearance process.

There have been moves by some banks towards a shorter clearance for checks payable between their different branches. Companies selecting a bank or reviewing their existing bank relationships should consider clearance times in assessing the quality of service provided by the bank.

Cash Collection: International Banking

Many companies trade internationally, buying and selling abroad or trading through business units and branches in other countries. Cash managers in these companies need to know

- the methods for making payments to foreign suppliers
- the methods for collecting payments from foreign customers
- the domestic banking system in the countries where they have operations.

Foreign Payments

It is important to realize that, with occasional exceptions, payments must be settled in the country of the currency of payment. Dollar payments must be cleared in New York, and go through the US clearing process. Similarly, sterling payments must be settled in London, and go through the UK banking-clearing system.

An exception is the London dollar clearing system that is used for some high-value dollar clearing in the London market. This clearing process is operated by APACS (Association for Payment Clearing Services) and member banks operate the clearing process by settling net transfers between the dollar accounts they hold with each other. Even with this system, the accounting for dollar transfers is carried out in New York.

The implementation of the Euro is expected to greatly simplify and accelerate the settlement procedure within participant countries. A key feature of the Economic and Monetary Union (EMU) will be the wide range of methods making and receiving Euro payments that will be available to banks. It is not clear how the banks will respond: some will continue to be payment banks; that is members of one or more Euro payment systems and offering correspondent banking services to third parties. Other banks may adopt one or more of the following alternative courses.

- Continue to use correspondent banking but select one correspondent in a single center with which to hold their main Euro account to receive Euro from and pay Euro to any of the 15 EU countries.
- Retain the present architecture, at least for a time, of an account with a correspondent in each of a number of countries so that funds are paid and received domestically, in the local payment systems.
- Make their own payments directly so that the services of a correspondent are no longer needed, via one or more of the several net and gross payment systems that will become available, including the linked TARGET network of RTGS (real time global settlement systems). Payments could be made directly either through local membership of those systems or remote membership from another center.

Because of this variety, banks will need to ensure that their systems can handle alternative ways of paying Euro and also that the Euro together with national currency units can be paid and received in a number of different countries until full monetary unification is achieved in 2002.

Example 1
Zug, a Swiss company, makes a payment in Swiss francs to Baker, a UK company. Baker banks with a large UK clearing bank that has branches in Switzerland.

Baker can arrange for its UK bank to collect the payment from Zug's bank. This will happen in Switzerland, with Romeo's bank transferring the funds to a Swiss branch of the UK bank. Baker will be notified in the UK that the Swiss branch is holding the francs on its behalf. This is illustrated overleaf.

Example: Payment from Abroad in a Foreign Currency

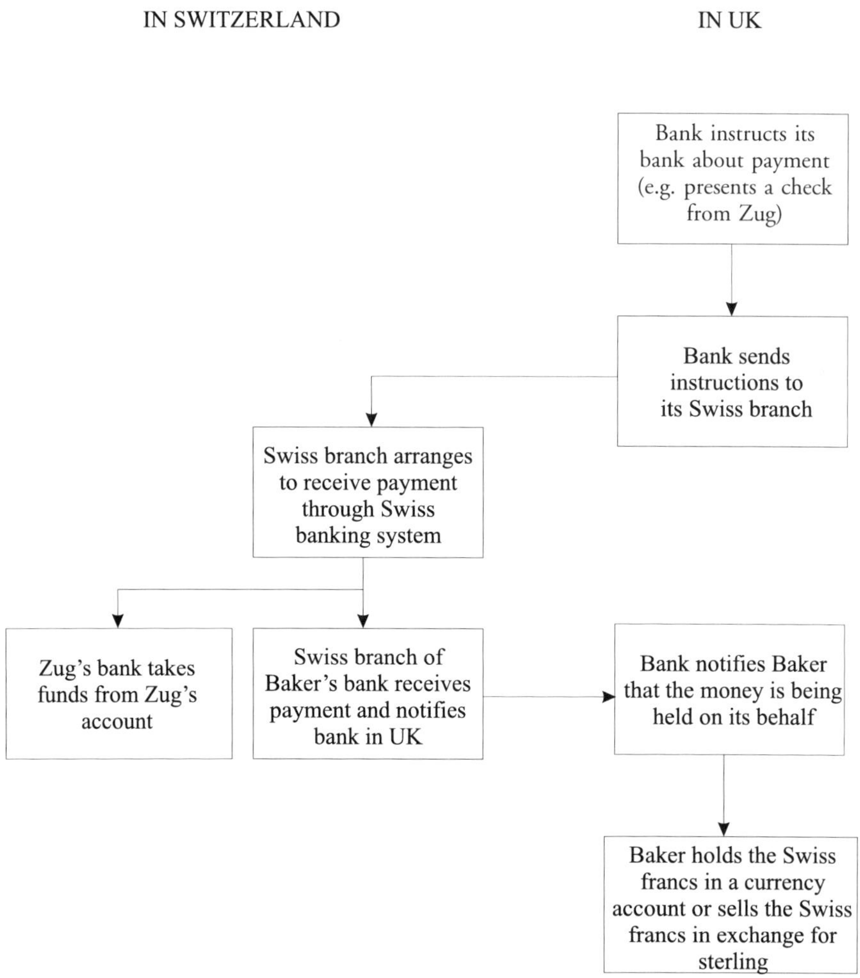

There is no movement of currency between Switzerland and the US. The francs stay in Switzerland with the branch of Baker's bank there. If Baker has a foreign currency account with its bank in the US, the funds would still be held with the branch in Switzerland. Alternatively, Baker could sell the currency to its bank, in which case its dollar account will be credited with the sale proceeds, and its funds will now be in the US.

Example 2
Victor, a US company, wishes to make a payment in Turkish lira to Tango, a Turkish company. Victor's bank in the US has an office in Istanbul.

Victor must arrange through its bank to have Turkish lira available in its Istanbul office to make the payment, perhaps by buying them from the bank in exchange for dollars. The lira would then be paid to Tango's bank by the Istanbul office of Victor's bank. The payment would take place in Turkey.

Correspondent Banks

Not all banks are international banks, and not all international banks have branches in every country or state. Because banks must provide an international service to customers there is a system of correspondent banks. A correspondent bank will perform a variety of services in one country on behalf of a bank (and its customers) in another country.

Correspondent banks maintain accounts with each other. If a bank has a correspondent bank in Japan, the bank will have a yen account with this bank. It will use this account to make yen payments and to receive yen receipts on behalf of its customers.

Similarly the Japanese bank will have a dollar account with the correspondent bank in the US, for dealing with dollar receipts or payments on behalf of its own customers.

Example
A US importer paying a supplier in Japan might pay by a check in dollars, in yen or in a third currency. The payment system will operate differently in each case.

If payment is by check in dollars, the check will be presented by the Japanese supplier to its bank in Japan. The bank will then send on the check by post to its correspondent bank that will obtain payment through the US clearing process. The dollar payment from the US importer's bank will be credited to the Japanese bank's dollar account that it maintains in the US with its correspondent bank. The Japanese bank will then notify its customer that the payment has been received.

Correspondent Banks: Payment in Dollars

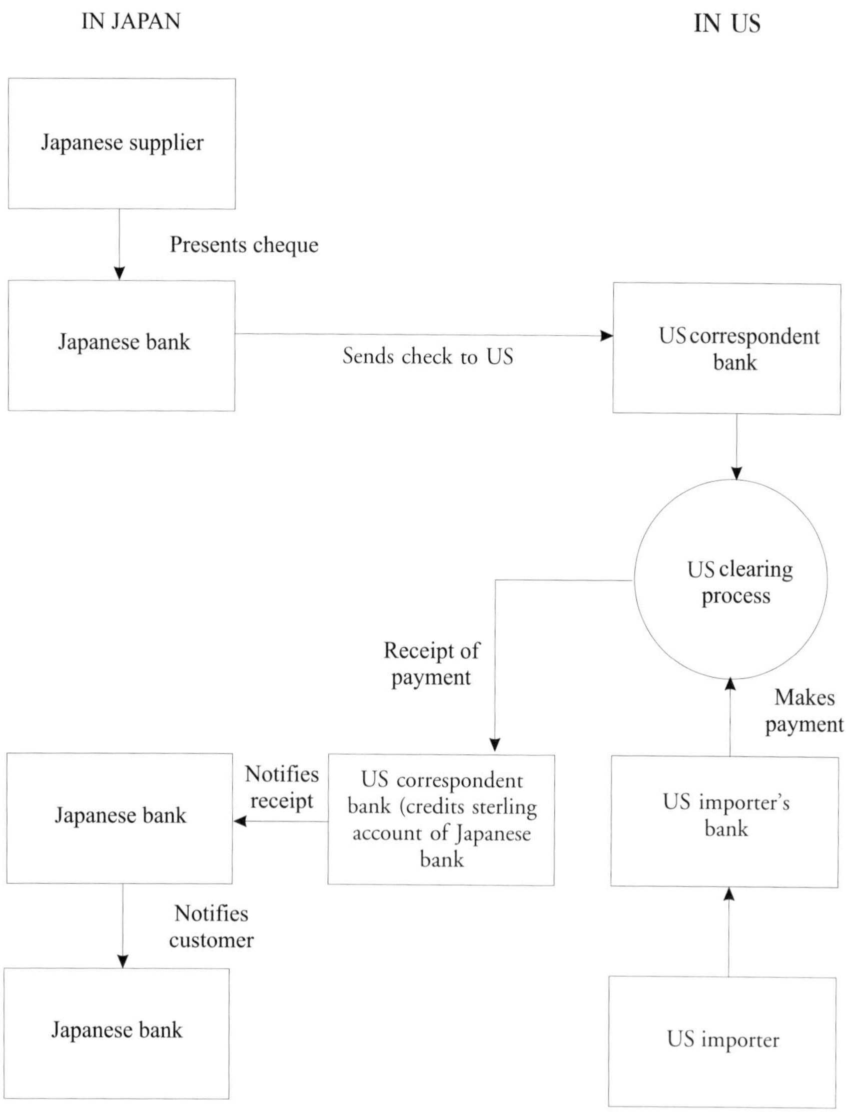

If payment by the US importer to the Japanese supplier is by a check in yen, the money transfer will take place in Japan, with the correspondent of the US bank making the payment to the Japanese supplier's bank.

Correspondent Banks: Payment in Yen

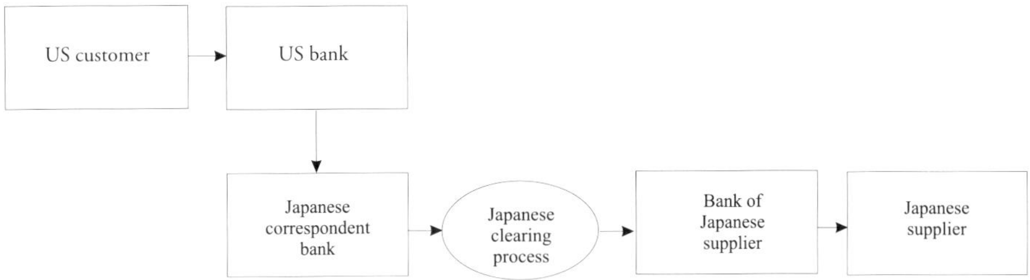

The US bank will have an account in yen with its Japanese correspondent, and this account will be debited when the payment is made.

If payment by the US importer to the Japanese supplier is by check in dollars, the money transfer will take place in the US, with payment between the correspondents of the US and Japanese banks.

Correspondent Banks: Payment in Dollars

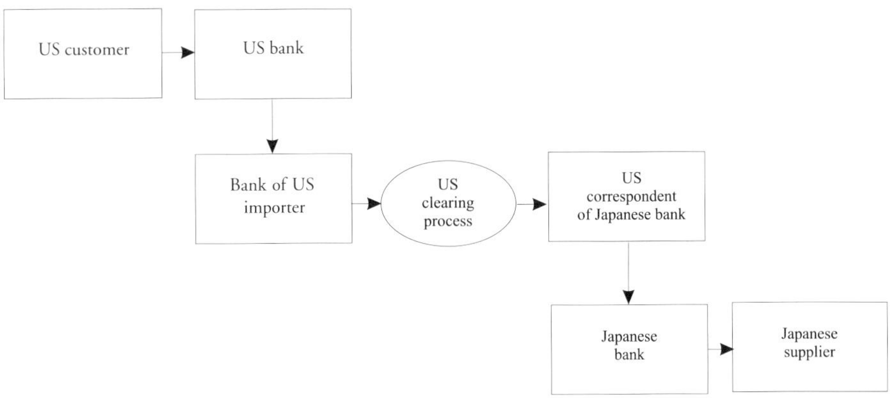

Nostro and Vostro Accounts

Correspondent banks keep accounts with each other in the other's domestic currency.

- The account held abroad in the domestic currency of the correspondent is called a *nostro account.* Money in a nostro account is a cash asset of the bank.
- The account held with a bank by its correspondent is a *vostro account.* Money in a vostro account, like any other deposit of a customer, is a liability of the bank.

Each bank keeps its own accounting records for cash assets held in nostro accounts and liabilities in vostro accounts. The nostro account of one correspondent should be a mirror image of the vostro account of the other.

Example

Beta Bank in the UK has a correspondent bank, Epsilon, in the US. Beta Bank's records show the following balances:

Nostro account with Epsilon Bank	$500,000
Vostro account with Epsilon Bank	£200,000

Beta Bank therefore has $500,000 in cash with Epsilon Bank that has £200,000 in cash with Beta.

If a customer of Epsilon Bank wishes to make a payment of $30,000 to a customer of Beta Bank, the money transfer will result in an increase in Beta Bank's nostro account balance to $530,000. If another customer of Epsilon Bank wishes to make a payment of £40,000 to a customer of Beta Bank, the money transfer will result in a decrease in the balance on the vostro account to £160,000. These changes are summarized in the table below.

Beta's Bank Records	**Opening Balance**	**Transfer**	**Closing Balance**
Nostro account in dollars with Epsilon Bank	$500,000	+$30,000	$530,000
Vostro account of Epsilon Bank in sterling	£200,000	–£40,000	£160,000

From Epsilon Bank's viewpoint, these payments would reduce the balance on its nostro account with Beta Bank to £160,000 and increase the balance on its vostro account with Beta to $530,000.

Methods of Settlement in International Trade

In international trade, payments are settled by check, banker's draft or electronic funds transfer between banks. Some payment methods, for example letters of credit, involve bills of exchange that are settled on presentation of the bill for payment at the appropriate bank and on the specified date, by means of funds transfer.

Instructions to transfer funds, either immediately or at a specified future date, can be sent to banks abroad. These instructions are sent by various methods, including mail transfer, wire transfer or via the SWIFT network.

The speed with which funds are transferred depends on the payment and settlement systems used. Funds transfers can be made immediately, whereas the collection of check payments can be very slow.

SWIFT

SWIFT (Society for Worldwide Interbank Financial Telecommunications) is an organization of international banks that provides an international message transmission system between member banks. Messages can be sent via the SWIFT network instructing a bank in another country to make a payment to a specified payee. The SWIFT network is particularly suitable when a fast payment method is required. For example, if a foreign customer wishes to pay a US supplier in dollars by immediate bank transfer, the instruction from the customer's bank to its US correspondent bank to make the payment could be sent by SWIFT.

On receipt of a SWIFT instruction to make a payment to a beneficiary, a bank is responsible for putting the payment into effect. Typically, payments will be settled through the correspondent banking system by debiting the account of the bank sending the payment instruction and crediting the account of the beneficiary or arranging for a transfer of funds to the beneficiary's bank.

A problem with the SWIFT system is its cost which must be borne by its members. Some European banks have been developing their own alternative systems because they regard SWIFT as too expensive.

The US Clearing System

Many foreign companies trade in the US, or with US customers or suppliers. The US banking system consists of many different banks, each licensed under either state law or federal law. Federal Reserve banks operate the US clearing system.

Banking regulations in the US are fairly restrictive although there has been a loosening of controls. The McFadden Act forbids inter-state banking, so that in principle the activities of any bank should be restricted to one state. However, with the plethora of credit problems and bank failures during the 1980s, the Federal Reserve Board has in some cases permitted the takeover of ailing banks by larger healthier banks who are willing to take the loss in order to expand beyond the state line, thereby avoiding the need for taxpayer funded bailouts. This trend has resulted in the formation of large new super regionals such as NationsBank. It has also encouraged the mergers of Travelers Group with Citicorp and the New York Club of the Manufacturers Hanover-Chemical-Chase Manhattan menage à trios. There are some regional pacts, for example in New England, that enable banks to operate across state lines. There is a continuing movement towards liberalizing US banking laws, but their number is still relatively large (over 9,000) when compared to the universal banks in Europe or Canada. While the days of universal banking by any single bank across the US are getting closer, they are probably still distant.

Because of the large number of banks that could be used to originate dollar payments, there is a danger of inefficiency and slow clearing; however, measures have been taken to ensure that checks are cleared quickly and bank float time is fairly short.

Checks

Checks must be moved physically from the bank where the check is presented for payment to the paying bank, and the clearing method used depends on which banks are involved. Major banks in the same geographical area will use a local clearing system; in other cases, clearing will be done through a Federal Reserve bank and will take up to three days.

Wire Transfers

Wire transfers can be used for high-value payments, to give same-day value to the payee. Payment instructions will be initiated from the customer to the paying bank, by telephone, fax or computer, and transmitted to the receiving bank using FedWire (for domestic transfers), CHIPS or SWIFT.

FedWire

This is a US government-owned system for funds transfer, operated through the Federal Reserve Bank. Each commercial bank maintains a reserve account at its nearest Fed and same-day transfers are made between these accounts.

If a customer of Chase Manhattan in New York wishes to make a high-dollar value, same-day transfer to a company that is the customer of Bank of America in California, the customer will make the FedWire transfer to Bank of America. Chase Manhattan will debit its customer's account and Bank of America will credit its customer's account with same-day value. The interbank transfer of funds will be settled between the banks by crediting the account of Bank of America and debiting the account of Chase Manhattan at their local Fed.

CHIPS (Clearinghouse Interbank Payments System)

This is owned by the New York Clearinghouse Association, and is a system for sending US dollar payment instructions electronically. It is used primarily for international payments. CHIPS payment instructions give same-day value to the recipient. Member banks maintain CHIPS settlement accounts. On receipt of a CHIPS instruction from another bank to make a payment to a beneficiary, the bank receiving the instruction will make an accounting book entry to debit the account of the paying bank and credit the account of the beneficiary.

Electronic Payments

These can be made through the Automated Clearing House (ACH) that is similar to BACS in the UK. The customer sends payment instructions to the bank on magnetic tape or via a terminal. The recipient of the payment obtains next-day value.

Lockbox

The lockbox collection service is also used to speed up the US payments system. A lockbox can be used for collecting payments in US dollars from several customers in a particular state or region. A company opens up a lockbox with a bank. Customers are asked to send payments to the bank, specifying the lockbox number. Mail sent to the lockbox is opened by the bank that processes the checks and sends them for clearing through the most appropriate route. Lockbox services are expensive, and the benefit of faster collection time should exceed the cost of the service to justify their use.

Delays in International Payments

The float time with international payments can be very long, for various reasons.

- The clearing system in the country concerned might be very slow. Collections must sometimes go through the clearing system of two countries.

- Time can be lost in moving checks physically from one country to another, when the check must go back to its country of origin for clearing.
- Processing documentation associated with a payment can take time. Banks often will process transactions slowly when it is essential to ensure that the documents are correct, especially in cases where the bank could be held responsible for any administrative error.
- Even immediate transfers can be delayed by the differing time zones of banking centers. SWIFT messages can be sent at any time of day, but they will not be acted on if the banks are closed in the country to which the message is going.
- The problem of float is particularly acute for exporters who receive payments by check or banker's draft. If the collection of payments is through correspondent banks the collection process could be slow because of the administrative procedures involved.

Delays within the European Union

Checks are widely used in all EU countries. Bank transfers are also used extensively. Float time for checks can be fairly short. In Germany, for example, clearance time for checks within the same bank is one to two days. In Spain, check clearance can vary from one day for payments within the same branch of the same bank, to five days for payments between different banks in different towns.

The Italian banking system has been particularly slow, although it is improving. Clearance delays can be very long. Some Italian companies have made arrangements with their bank for fixed-value dates for checks received and paid in. The bank credits the company's account on the fixed date, regardless of whether it has received the funds from the paying bank. Advice delay is also long in Italy; a customer might not be informed about payments received until a month or so later.

Summary

Companies making or receiving payments in other countries should ask their bank for information about the clearing system and normal methods of payment within that country. If they are concerned about the delay in collecting a payment from abroad, they should ask their bank for an estimate of what the float time might be. They might be surprised at just how long this might be.

Reviewing Cash Collection and Payments

It is always worth checking bank charges for receipts and payments. However, for many companies, bank fees and commissions for cash transmission are not a large cost item, and there is little scope for cost cutting by switching banks or renegotiating bank charges.

More significant savings in bank charges are likely to come from reductions in bank float time, and therefore lower overdraft interest charges. Alternatively, shorter float time will increase a cash surplus, and provide the opportunity for higher income from short-term investment. Financial controllers or treasury managers ought to monitor the causes of float within their organization, with a view to reducing float time at a reasonable cost.

However, it is worth remembering that if reductions in float time benefit the company, they will create a cost for either the company's customers or its bank. By obtaining value for funds more quickly

- customers either lose their money sooner, or
- the banking system loses the free use of the funds that are in the process of being cleared.

Similarly, if a company seeks a longer float time for its payments transactions, it will create a cost for its suppliers, its bank, or its suppliers' banks.

Interest Cost of Float Time

A company could take action to reduce the float, but such measures could also increase bank transaction charges. The cost of quicker cash collection needs to be justified by the size of the benefits. The benefits of shorter float times for receivables are higher interest income or lower overdraft charges, because cash will be received into a bank account sooner.

Interest charges for an overdraft are linked to the bank's base rate or to a money market rate such as LIBOR, (London Inter Bank Offered Rate). In the US and UK interest is charged at a single rate on the daily borrowing, but in other countries there are variations in the basis for charging overdraft interest. For example, two interest rates could be used, or interest could be charged on a combination of average daily balance and peak balance during the period.

There will be occasions when a receipt for good value is anticipated late in the day, typically if the payment is arriving via an international transmission system. In such circumstances the cash manager could anticipate the receipt and pre-invest the funds in the money markets or in a deposit, interest-bearing, account rather than in a non- or low-interest-bearing currency account.

In the event that the payment fails to arrive, an overdraft facility should be available to cover the pre-invested amount to ensure that the company is not in default to its bank. Such action could result in a net loss to the company that is the difference between the investment rate and the overdraft-borrowing rate. In the long run, the benefits of such pre-investment activity should significantly outweigh the cost of the occasional delayed receivable.

Managing Float Time

Float time for receipts from customers can be shortened by reducing transmission delay, lodgment delay, clearance delay or advice delay. A company can achieve reductions by more efficient cash management or through the agreement of its customers or bank.

Reducing Transmission Delay

It could be argued that a company should seek to increase the float time for payments, by using a slow transmission system or insisting on a payment method that requires longer clearance. More likely, however, this attitude leads to the demand for longer credit, or the deliberate delay of payments beyond the due date. Although it is quite common business practice, the delay of payments to suppliers is not recommended, and should not be a long-term solution for improving cash management.

Reducing Lodgment Delay

To control lodgment delay, all checks and cash should be deposited on the day of receipt. Occasional delays in banking checks might not be too costly, but in-built procedural delays should not be allowed. For example, if a company receives fairly substantial payments by check daily through the post, they should be banked daily. A company that has a policy of banking checks once a week is guilty of inefficiency, increasing float time by up to five working days.

Reducing Clearance Delay

A company can try to negotiate with its bank for shorter clearance delays for money receipts. A bank may not be willing to offer better clearance times, unless the company is a valued customer with a substantial volume of banking business.

It is more likely, however, especially for the clearance of domestic payments, that to achieve shorter clearance delays, different methods of payment/settlement would be required. There should be

- a review process of current settlement methods
- an assessment of alternative methods
- an arrangement whereby, if better methods could be used, a process of negotiating acceptance from customers.

The Review Process

A company should carry out an occasional review of the cash collection and payment methods that it uses. Current methods of collecting and making payments should be analyzed over time, according to the banking instrument used, how the payments/collections were routed and the banks used.

A part of the analysis should be to look at the value dating of collections/payments, and the duration and the size of float. Bank fees and charges also should be considered, together with the cost of overdraft funds (or the income obtainable from short-term deposits). The nature of any agreements about payment methods between the company and its suppliers and customers should be reviewed.

Domestic Payments

Alternative cash collection payment methods could be considered. A bank will probably be willing to give advice, especially if it has a good working relationship with the company. The bank *might* even be willing to reduce its clearance time for checks, and give the company good value for its funds a day or two earlier than at present.

Float time for the receipt of domestic payments might be reduced by encouraging customers to use a particular method or methods of payment. Customers could be invited, for example, to make regular payments by standing order or direct debit that are more reliable than payment by check. However, customers could insist on paying by check.

Automated payments

Automated payments are quicker than paper methods of payment, and can be value-dated, ensuring that payment is made/received on a specified date. Automated payments systems include those previously described. Another system is EFTPOS (Electronic Funds Transfer at the Point of Sale), a debit-transfer system with enormous potential as an alternative to checks. A customer pays for goods by debit card with payment details transmitted to the customer's bank from a terminal at the retailer's checkout desk. Funds transfer could be instantaneous but is currently value-dated to correspond with normal check-clearing times to avoid penalizing customers who use this method of payment rather than checks. Use of debit cards is assuming increasing importance. In France, debit cards, known as smart cards, with an embedded microchip for added security have become the primary means of secure payment and the use of personal checks is declining.

International Payments

For international check clearing, it is difficult to monitor the normal bank float time accurately because collection times can be quite long. Any lengthy delays, or increases in average delays from one period to the next, should be queried with the bank. It might be possible to negotiate short float times for international checks.

For international payments, a customer might agree to pay by telex transfer or the SWIFT network rather than by check, and the transfer of funds can be value-dated. The customer might be given longer credit and could therefore benefit. The supplier would get the benefit of funds on the specified value date. Both customer and supplier could benefit from a reduction in bank float time, although bank charges for telex transfers and SWIFT messages are higher than for international collection of check payments.

Exporters to some countries will require payment to be guaranteed by a letter of credit obtained from a bank. In a letter of credit, the bank promises to make a payment to the exporter on the debtor's behalf, provided that the exporter presents certain documents within a specified time to a specified bank.

The exporting company should try to ensure that payment with a letter of credit is obtained at a bank in its own country, and not in the customer's country, in order to reduce the delay in receiving payment.

- With *confirmed* irrevocable letters of credit (CILCs), the undertaking by the debtor's bank to make the payment is supported by a bank usually in the exporter's own country, and payment normally will be arranged in the exporter's own country.

- With *unconfirmed* irrevocable letters of credit (ILCs), the exporter is relying on the undertaking of the debtor's bank in another country, and arranging payment at a bank in the exporter's own country might be more difficult. Some exporters will refuse to deliver goods unless a letter of credit is confirmed.

Negotiating the Payment Method

Before alternative methods of payment are selected, they should be discussed with the suppliers and customers who would be affected. The company's bank also should be notified, and bank charges should be negotiated for any new collection or payment methods that are put in place.

There may be only restricted scope for changing methods of payment from customers. Some companies must be able to offer a variety of payment methods to their customers. If customers are the general public (utilities, retailers) it could be essential to offer different payment methods to attract custom and make it easy for customers to pay. Not all retail companies take this view, however, and refuse payments by external credit cards. For business customers within the same country, it is standard practice to accept payment by check, and although other methods of payment can be arranged, it would be difficult to refuse payments by check.

Negotiating a method of payment as a condition of the sale can be appropriate for:

- large-value payments, where the company wants to be certain of receiving cleared funds on a specific date, or before fulfilling the contract, for example before delivering the goods
- export sales, because some payment methods will offer a much shorter float time.

It is common and acceptable practice to negotiate the method of payment as part of the contract with exports to many countries. This is less likely in the EU, where sales on credit and payment by check or banker's draft are common.

Reducing Advice Delay

A company could lose the opportunity to use or invest funds simply because it is unaware that it has the cleared funds in its account. If so, this is careless cash management. Information about cleared balances can be obtained either by telephoning the bank or by installing a cash-management reporting system, with a terminal linked up to the bank's information systems. The cleared balance on the account as at the end of the previous day can be obtained early the next morning. This is discussed in greater detail in the chapter on electronic banking systems.

An estimate can be made of the cleared balance on the account as at the end of the current day, because the bank will know what checks will be cleared on that day, and can inform the customer. By making adjustments for any expected cabled transfers of funds in the day, the company can forecast with reasonable accuracy what the day's cleared balance will be and make suitable arrangements for the investment of any surplus cash.

If a large corporate customer negotiates specific float times with its bank, it can predict its cleared balances with reasonable accuracy over a slightly longer period of the next two or three days. When it lodges checks with its bank for payment it will know that value will be received in a specified number of days.

Summary

Delays in collecting cash can be expensive, and if a company's cash collection systems are inefficient, the costs could be high. However, improvements in cash collection are likely to cost money and could also affect good business relationships with suppliers or customers.

Even so, a company should monitor its cash collection, and try to identify inefficiencies and scope for improvements. Export sales are a particular area where reductions in float time could be significant.

5

The Customer-Bank Relationship

One of the functions of cash management is to put in place suitable banking arrangements for cash balances. Banks can offer a number of alternative systems, and companies should select a system that meets their requirements at a suitable cost. The relationship between a company and its bank or banks can be important for ensuring that satisfactory banking arrangements are established and operated.

Relationship Banking and Transaction Banking

Many companies deal with more than one bank, but a distinction is made between

- relationship banking, and
- transaction banking.

In *relationship banking* a company, or large business unit within a company, builds up a relationship with one bank, sometimes two or three, for most of its banking services. In contrast, *transaction banking* means that a company obtains its banking services for a specific transaction from any of several different banks, opting for the bank offering the cheapest cost or best dealing rate.

The main reasons for transaction banking are:

- Borrowing. Companies that borrow heavily often will need to approach many banks to obtain sufficient loans at an acceptable rate of interest. This can be either via a series of bilateral (company to one bank) loans or via syndicated loans that are a borrowing arrangement between a company and a panel of several banks.

- Obtaining the best price for a specific banking service, such as borrowing, short-term investments and foreign currency transactions.
- When dealing with specialized products in which a particular bank has a specialization or competitive edge over other banks.

In practice, a company might opt for relationship banking for some banking services and transaction banking for others. However, for efficient cash management some form of relationship banking makes the most sense.

As a general rule, for cash handling and cash transmission, a company should try to keep the number of counterparty commercial banks and bank accounts to a minimum. Even very large companies stick to just one or two banks, although with many accounts at various branches, perhaps.

The simplest banking arrangement is to have a single account for the company, but this is not always administratively convenient. When a company collects cash at various locations it can be convenient to have a separate account at each location. In addition, sometimes it is useful to have special purpose accounts, such as an account exclusively for the payment of dividends.

In large companies, different accounts could be set up for historical or organizational reasons. If a new subsidiary company is acquired, the subsidiary might be allowed, for convenience, to maintain the relationship with its pre-acquisition bank.

The accounts department of a large business unit often will have the freedom to operate its own bank account, choose its own bank and establish its own local relationship with this bank. This local bank could be a different branch of the same bank the rest of the company uses, or perhaps a different bank altogether. However in large companies with a centralized treasury department, the selection tends to be controlled centrally, with business awarded to a relationship bank. Head office might carry out a periodic tender for the commercial banking needs of the company and decide whether the company as a whole should switch its business to another bank.

Local Currency Accounts

Using a local currency account is an alternative to maintaining a foreign currency account with a domestic bank in the company's own country. For example, a US company might choose to open an account with a bank in Japan to process its multiple transactions in order to reduce bank charges. This going-native option is now more widely used than in the past, and it increases the number of relationship banks with which the company deals.

Advantages of Relationship Banking

Relationship banking has some important advantages for both the bank and its corporate customer, especially in an economic downturn when over-borrowed companies struggle to refinance maturing loans and to extend their facilities. It can help to deal with one bank that knows the company well instead of several banks that are not very familiar with the company's business and are likely to be less sympathetic to its requests.

A bank might prefer to view its business in terms of the overall profitability of a particular customer rather than in terms of the profitability of each individual transaction. As a result, the bank might be willing to offer low margin lending if it can sell other profitable services to the company in the future. Or, it could reduce its commercial banking transaction charges to retain preferential supplier status for other, higher-margin products. It is not unusual for a bank to charge an established customer a quarterly flat-rate fee for a current account service because the profits or losses on these are negligible compared with the benefits of providing other more lucrative services.

However, competition in retail banking has led to a change of thinking with much greater emphasis placed on customer service. Banks also place greater emphasis on the need for each of their services (products) to be profitable. As a general rule, banks are now more likely to want a satisfactory margin on all their products, and preferential pricing deals to favored customers will be on the basis of transaction volume for each particular service.

A company should benefit from relationship banking by getting a better quality of service, including advice and assistance with complex transactions, such as international money dealings. The bank will appoint one or more client relations officers with the responsibility for looking after a particular corporate customer and the bank's relationship with it. The client relations officer will be able to respond quickly to queries, and identify specialists within the bank to deal with particular problems. For example, a company that wants to buy or sell a large quantity of foreign currency in a one-off transaction could ask its client relations officer if the bank will offer finer rates than usual for the transaction, in view of its size. The client relations officer could put the customer directly in touch with the bank's main currency dealing room. The officer also is likely to extend the customer's borrowing facilities (up to a limit) without the need for higher authority.

The bank should be able to build up a good understanding of the company and its requirements, possibly identifying useful extra services about which the company is unaware.

A single relationship bank simplifies the cash management process by concentrating the banking flows and various account balances of the company within one bank and therefore within one computerized monitoring system.

Bank Charges

One objective of cash management should be to keep bank charges within reason. It is not just borrowing costs and interest rates that matter.

Bank charges are levied quarterly and are negotiable between a company and its bank. Even if a company uses only one clearing bank it might be worth shopping around occasionally to find out what charges other banks offer and complaining when a particular charge is considered too high. Cash managers, out of interest alone, might wish to compare the tariffs of other banks with those of their own bank. Reasonable savings could be achieved by shopping around and complaining loudly enough. For a company with annual turnover of several million pounds, bank charges can be as low as a few thousand pounds per annum, although costs obviously will vary with the number of cash inflow/outflow transactions and the use of other banking services.

A charging structure could include:

- *Overdraft interest*, usually at a margin above the bank's base rate. Interest would be chargeable on a daily basis and payable perhaps each month, quarter or half year.
- *An itemized charge* for each type of banking transaction.
- *Turnover charge.* A charge levied as a percentage of the value of entries on the periodic bank statement.
- *Minimum balance or compensating balance.* A bank might specify that a certain amount of cash should be on deposit as an interest-free balance in compensation for lower transaction charges.
- *Notional interest credit.* Notional interest might be credited to the company's account, to set against transaction charges, based on the average cleared credit balance in the period on the company's current account.

Banks might try to simplify their tariffs to smaller business customers by specifying the charges for regular items, and suggesting that specific charges for other services can be provided on request.

Example

A newly acquired subsidiary of a group of companies, Gamma Inc., is switching its bank account to the local branch of the group's relationship bank, Omega Bank. The subsidiary will retain control over its banking arrangements, because of its geographical distance from group head office. Its annual turnover is around $2.5 million.

The customer liaison officer for Omega Bank simplifies the tariff structure for the new customers in the following letter.

OMEGA BANK

14 East 17th Street
New York, NY

Dear Mr. Jones

Gamma Inc.

I was very pleased to meet you a few days ago and, as promised, am writing to supply details regarding the opening of a bank account for the above company.

We shall be very pleased to operate a bank account for Gamma Inc., and the account number details are as follows:

Current account	1234557
Interest-bearing account	7655433

As you will see, both a current and an interest-bearing account have been opened.

As discussed, we shall operate your account under the same terms and conditions that apply to the rest of the group. For your information this is activity-based and, at present, rebated by 20% as follows:

Checks paid and other chargeable debit entries	60¢
Sundry credits	85¢
Checks collected	30¢

Other charges for special services are available on request.

Interest terms for the interest-bearing account are as follows:

$100,000 plus	– 6.0%
$ 10,000 plus	– 5.5%
$ 2,500 plus	– 1.0%
$ 2,500 or less	– Nil

These rates are available for all monies and are repayable without notice to the current account. There are other lodgment products that may be applicable to the new company because cash flow is intended to be positive. These include a 14-day notice account. We shall be pleased to advise you further when specific details of the surplus monies available are known.

Yours sincerely,

W Roberts

Organization of Banking Arrangements

The responsibilities for expenditures and cash management either will be centralized or decentralized within a company or group of companies.

Within Europe, multinational companies have been moving away from autonomous subsidiaries within each country towards an integrated pan-European organization for their operations, concentrating their activities on just one or two major sites. As a consequence, the cash management function is likely to become more centralized.

What does centralization mean?

The centralization of cash management within a multinational does not mean that all payments are made from head office. Local credit checking, customer invoicing and other daily routines are a controllership function, that will be made by a local accounts office, although broad policy for these items might be decided centrally. With centralization, information about cash or cash requirements is given to the central treasury that can then decide the optimal method of allocating available cash and meeting funding requirements. Some treasury operations might be delegated to a local level, such as the investment of short-term cash surpluses (say for seven days or less). Central treasury would take decisions about the opening and closing of bank accounts, and transfers between accounts.

Responsibility for expenditures is not the same as responsibility for cash management. Managers could be empowered to authorize spending up to a certain limit, but the task of signing checks, monitoring cash balances or arranging overdraft facilities could lie elsewhere.

Cash management responsibilities could be divided between head office and cashier departments within each business unit or subsidiary. For example, centralized items for which the group treasurer is responsible could include

- bank relationships
- group cash management (through head office bank accounts)
- currency exposure management
- funding management.

- payments for certain items (e.g. expenditures above a certain value).

Items delegated to the financial controller in the business unit could include:

- day-to-day cash receipts
- day-to-day cash payments
- control over float times and working capital in the business unit or profit center.

Each business unit could have its own bank account, but preferably with the same bank as other business units in the group operating in the same country.

Advantages and Disadvantages of Central Cash Management

The coordination of cash transfers and cash balances by a central office should help to minimize borrowing costs and optimize investment returns, by minimizing overdrafts and using cash surpluses more efficiently.

With head office control over payments for major expenditure items, the group's cash needs will be less susceptible to large and unexpected payments. Subsidiaries would be unable, without giving proper advance warning, to agree payments for large contracts.

By coordinating the banking requirements for the whole group, a centralized cash management team is more likely to negotiate lower charges or a better level of service from its banks. Economies of scale might be possible, with expert cash managers in a central location able to arrange larger volume transactions at a lower cost.

A disadvantage of centralized control over cash management is the tension that might be created between remote head-office specialists and operations managers on the ground. For example, central treasury refusing to pay suppliers on the date requested by a business unit could lead to accusations by the business unit managers that supplier goodwill is being jeopardized. If managers in business units are not responsible for cash, they will be more aware of operational problems than cash management issues.

In a group of companies, cash management responsibilities normally should be shared between head office and local business units, to obtain the benefits of centralization without losing a sense of responsibility for cash at a local level. If the division of responsibilities can be properly organized, a company can reap the benefits of a dual focus on cash control.

Where business units have their own bank accounts, but the responsibility for borrowing and investing cash is centralized in head office, the company or group will have to establish a configuration for its banking arrangements.

Bank Account Configurations

Bank account configurations are the systems by which companies with more than one bank account organize the banking arrangements for their cash balances, cash inflows and outflows, their overdraft, borrowing and the use of surplus cash for investment.

The chosen design for a company's banking configuration will depend on negotiations with its bank, as well as the organizational structure, size and culture of the company or group of companies concerned.

- What are its business units?
- Where are they located?
- How large are they and what is their annual turnover?
- What is the degree of centralization/decentralization of authority within the company?

The configuration chosen by a particular company can reduce costs or improve income fairly substantially by

- reducing overdraft balances and so overdraft interest costs.
- using surplus cash more efficiently by investing at a better rate of interest.
- reducing foreign exchange exposures.

This is achieved by cross funding between the various accounts.

Configurations where a company has more than one current account involve netting, and cash pooling and concentration accounts. Netting is a system for minimizing and coordinating money transfers between bank accounts. Pooling and concentration accounts are systems for optimizing the use of cash balances.

7

Netting

With a netting arrangement, a company or group has two or more bank accounts, with money transfers between accounts in either direction. Typically, there will be a separate account for each business unit or subsidiary company. The transfer of money between accounts could arise from payments for trading between business units or subsidiaries. There could be intra-group payments for dividends or interest on loans, or perhaps for other transactions. The bank accounts could be in the same country and the same currency, but they could be in different countries (foreign subsidiaries) and different currencies.

The concept of netting is that instead of making regular payments for every transaction, from one account to another and back again, only net amounts owed are paid between accounts, and at regular intervals, every month perhaps, or every quarter.

Bilateral Netting

The simplest netting arrangement is between two bank accounts in the same currency. These could be the separate accounts of two subsidiary companies that carry on some trade between themselves. Each company will owe the other for goods or services bought on credit, and at the same time will be owed for goods or services supplied on credit. Under a netting arrangement, there would be a single payment, at regular monthly or quarterly intervals, from one subsidiary to the other. The payment would be from the subsidiary owing more to the one owing less, and for the net difference. Amounts owed, but in dispute, can be held over until the next payment date.

Example 1

Alpha Group has two subsidiaries, Beta and Gamma. Beta and Gamma trade regularly between themselves, and each has its own bank account. A bilateral netting scheme is operated with net payments settled on the last working day of each month.

At the end of March the amounts owed by and to each subsidiary were as follows:

Beta
Its sales ledger shows $820,000 owed by Gamma, and its purchase ledger shows $500,000 owing to Gamma.

Gamma
Its sales ledger shows $500,000 owed by Beta, and its purchase ledger shows $800,000 owing to Beta.

There is an item in dispute for sales from Beta to Gamma of $20,000. It is agreed to hold over this disputed item to the next payment date at the end of April.

Analysis

At the end of March, there will be a single net payment, perhaps by check, from Gamma to Beta of $300,000.

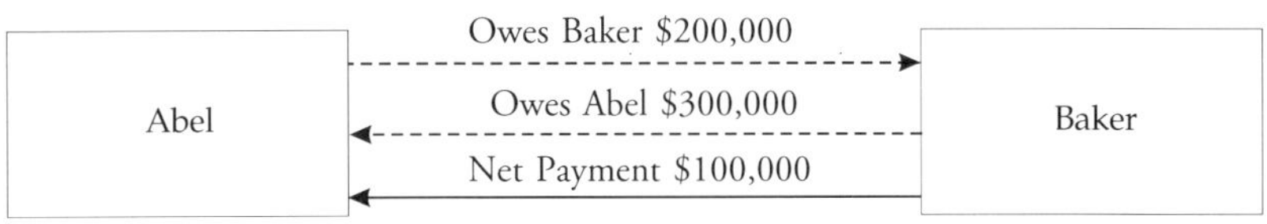

A further possible advantage of a bilateral netting arrangement is the cash discipline it helps to impose on the managers of each subsidiary. Subsidiaries are required to settle the debts between themselves regularly. If formal netting arrangements did not exist, and one of the subsidiaries had cash-flow difficulties, its management might try to alleviate the cash problems by delaying payments to a fellow subsidiary. This would have the effect of spreading the cash flow problem around the group, instead of concentrating it in the subsidiary where the problem occurs.

Bilateral netting can be established where the two subsidiaries and bank accounts are in different countries and different currencies. A system would be necessary for establishing the exchange rate between the two currencies. This could be the spot exchange rate at the time the net payment is agreed. Alternatively, the group might apply a standard exchange rate each month that would have to be reviewed and amended in the event that market exchange rates altered substantially. The subsidiary owed the higher amount would be paid in its own currency, and either the subsidiary owing the money or the group's central treasury (on behalf of the subsidiary) would arrange a foreign exchange transaction to obtain the currency to make the payment.

Example 2

Delta Group has two subsidiaries, Abel in the US and Baker in the UK. Abel and Baker trade regularly between themselves, each invoicing the other in its own currency. A bilateral netting arrangement is operated, with net payments on the 15th of each month (or the next working day).

On May 15, Abel is owed $690,000 by Baker, and Baker is owed £200,000 by Abel.

An exchange rate of $1.6 = £1 has been established for the May net payment.

Analysis

The net payment can be calculated in either currency, using the exchange rate $1.6 = £1.

	In dollars	**In sterling**
	$	£
Abel owes Baker	320,000	200,000
Baker owes Abel	690,000	431,250
Net: Baker owes Abel	370,000	231,250

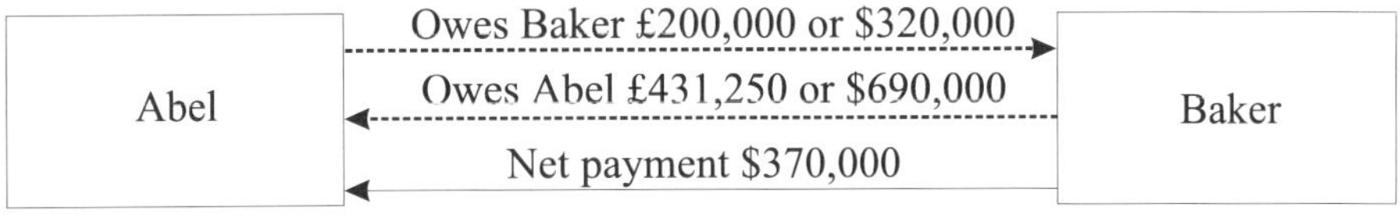

Because the net payment is due to Abel, a US subsidiary, the payment would be in dollars. Baker would purchase $370,000 in the FX markets, or ask head office to obtain $370,000 on its behalf, to make the payment. The actual exchange rate obtained might not be $1.6 unless a special arrangement has been agreed with the company's bank, and there could be an exchange gain or loss with the netting payment for either subsidiary.

Multilateral Netting

When a company has several subsidiaries, each with its own bank account, a series of bilateral netting arrangements could be operated. In practice it is likely that there will be multilateral netting when more than two bank accounts are involved. The same principles of netting apply, although the arrangements for net transfers are more complex than for bilateral netting. A central account at head office probably will be used to coordinate the net payment arrangements and determine what the net payments should be. Alternatively, a bank could provide the centralized control function over the netting payments.

There should be an agreed, regular date for netting payments, such as the last working day of each month, on which all amounts due are settled.

Multilateral Netting

WITHOUT MULTILATERAL NETTING

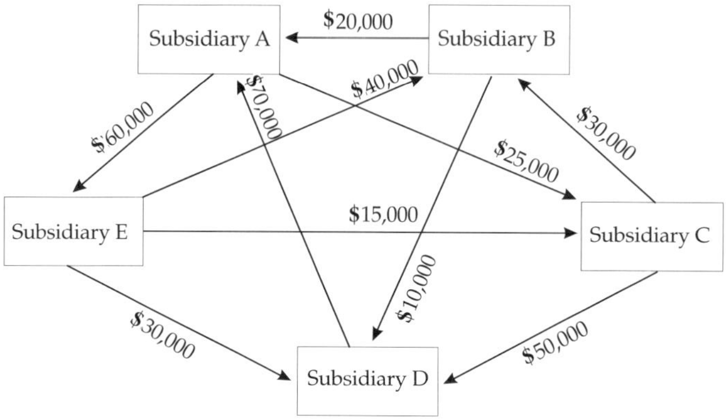

WITH MULTILATERAL NETTING

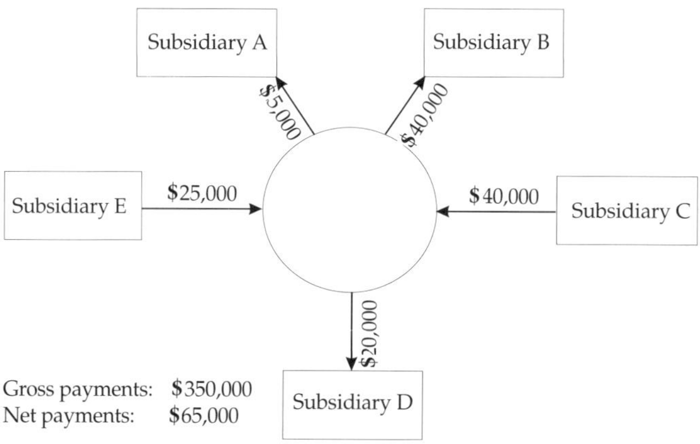

Gross payments: $350,000
Net payments: $65,000

Example

Indigo Group has four subsidiaries (Romeo, Sierra, Tango and Victor) that carry on some inter-company trading. Each has its own bank account. Multilateral netting arrangements operate, with payments made on the last Friday of each month for all amounts owing as at the previous Monday.

On Monday June 23, the sales ledgers and purchase ledgers for each subsidiary showed the following inter-company debts.

Accounts Records	Romeo	Sierra	Tango	Victor
	$	$	$	$
Sales Ledgers				
Owed by Romeo	–	40,000	200,000	–
Owed by Sierra	100,000	–	150,000	200,000
Owed by Tango	250,000	60,000	–	50,000
Owed by Victor	50,000	100,000	150,000	–
	400,000	200,000	500,000	250,000
Purchase ledgers				
Owing to Romeo	–	100,000	250,000	50,000
Owing to Sierra	40,000	–	60,000	100,000
Owing to Tango	200,000	150,000	–	150,000
Owing to Victor	Nil	200,000	50,000	–
	240,000	450,000	360,000	300,000
Net position	Owed 160,000	Owes 250,000	Owed 140,000	Owes 50,000

Analysis

There are just four bank accounts, and six payment routes between accounts. With bilateral netting between each pair of subsidiaries, there would be six net payments each month.

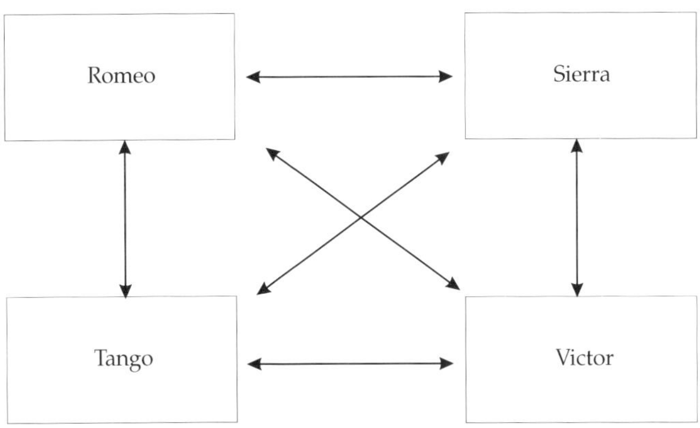

With multilateral netting, the number of payments can be reduced to one per bank account. The transfers would be totally under head-office control.

Netting payments could be arranged so that:

- Sierra pays central office $250,000
- Victor pays central office $50,000
- Romeo receives $160,000 from central office
- Tango receives $140,000 from central office

Just four money transfers will settle all inter-company debts.

In larger groups with more than four subsidiaries and bank accounts, multilateral netting can reduce intra-group money transfers appreciably, compared with bilateral netting arrangements.

Netting Banks

Companies can set up their own systems for netting, using an in-house computer model, based perhaps on a spreadsheet package such as Lotus or Supercalc. Some US and European banks offer a netting system that customers can lease or rent at a fee, and that provides the software for administering netting payments.

Third Party Netting

Although netting systems are primarily for settling of debts between companies in the same group, third parties can be included within a system. If an external company buys regularly from some companies in the group and sells to others, it could be invited to join the netting arrangement, making payments to or receiving payments from the group's netting center at regular intervals, such as the end of every month.

Cross-Border Multilateral Netting Systems

A multilateral netting system can be operated between bank accounts in different countries and currencies, although it can be difficult to establish a system given the differences in banking practices and computer standards between countries. Such a system is for only a sophisticated cash-management operation. A netting system could be arranged where every month, each subsidiary would either make or receive just one payment to settle inter-company debts within the group.

A cross-border multilateral netting system should use a single common currency to measure the amounts owed. This avoids the complications of netting inter-company debts in a variety of currencies, and with an exchange rate having to be agreed between every currency within the system.

The group must have agreement from its bank for a netting system to operate, because the system could be workable only if the bank takes on some currency risk for a short period during which net payments are settled. Suppose, for example, that a US-based multinational has six subsidiaries that trade with each other regularly.

- US Inc
- UK Ltd
- Germany GmbH
- France SARL
- Netherlands BV
- Euro SARL

In a multilateral netting system with monthly settlements between subsidiaries, there will be six inter-company payments each month. This compares with 15 payments that would be needed if bilateral arrangements were established between each pair of subsidiaries.

Bilateral Links

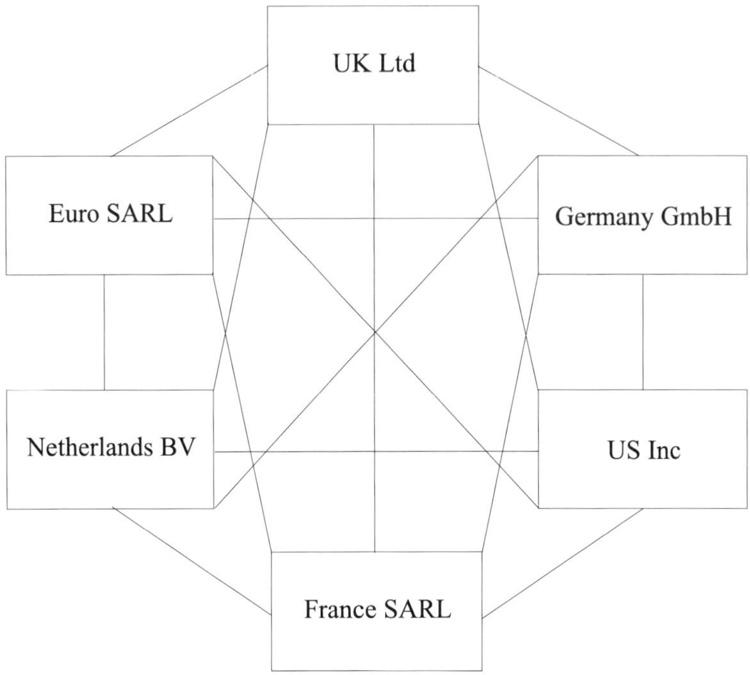

It can be arranged, for example, that on the fifth working day of every month netting payments will be made to clear outstanding balances as at the end of the previous month.

By the second working day of the month, agreement between subsidiaries about their inter-company debts could be reached, with debts denominated in the currency in which payment is due.

Suppose that in this example, the reference currency is Euro.

- All the outstanding debts between the subsidiaries in the Euro zone would be accounted for as Euros. Companies using Euros would not need any conversion into Euros.
- For companies in non-Euro countries such as the US, amounts will be converted into the common currency, the Euro, at a rate of exchange specified by the group's central treasury department, possibly the current spot rates.

Each subsidiary's net position then can be established: it should owe or be owed a net payment, expressed in Euros. These amounts can then be converted into the subsidiary's domestic currency, to provide a net amount payable or receivable in its domestic currency. For example, if the US subsidiary is owed a net amount of Euro100,000, its net payment receivable can be expressed in dollars.

Arrangements to make the net payments on the fifth working day of the month are not yet complete. To make or receive inter-company payments in the currency of each subsidiary, the group may need to buy or sell some currency at the spot rate on the foreign exchange markets.

This is where the cooperation of the company's bank becomes essential. The bank could now be asked to provide spot exchange rates for the estimated net payments between subsidiaries. These spot rates will differ from the rates provided by the group's central treasury and used for the netting calculations thus far.

The process of recalculating net payments should be done again, using the bank's quoted spot rates instead of central treasury's estimated rates. This should be done quickly, but it will take a little time to decide what the revised net payments should be. During this period of recalculating net payments, the bank would agree to hold its quoted exchange rates, even though spot market rates will be changing continuously. Net payments would then be established in sterling, converted into the appropriate currency for each subsidiary, and the required currency then bought or sold at the spot rates quoted by the bank in order to make the netting payments.

Subsidiaries that must make a netting payment will be instructed immediately by the company treasurer to pay the specified amount of currency to the bank. The bank will buy this currency in exchange for sterling, and will pay the sterling into the company's netting bank account. For subsidiaries receiving a netting payment, the company will buy the currency (spot) from the bank, paying for it out of the netting bank account. The bank will be instructed to transfer the currency to the specified accounts of the subsidiaries.

For currency transactions, value date is two working days after the transaction date; therefore the net receivers of payments will receive same-day value two working days later (i.e. in this example, on the fifth working day of the month).

The bank will buy and sell the actual quantities of currency in the netting payments, not the estimated quantities for which it quoted the spot rates. This means that there will be some foreign exchange gain or loss for the bank every month, although the bank would expect these to be relatively small.

These arrangements can seem complex, and an example involving just three subsidiaries and three currencies perhaps illustrates them more clearly.

Example
Worldwide Group has three subsidiaries, US Inc, UK Limited, and Germany GmbH. Each has a bank account in its own currency, and the three subsidiaries trade with each other regularly. A multilateral netting scheme operates whereby on the seventh working day of each month, all outstanding debts between them as at the end the previous month are settled.

The following outstanding debts at end June were agreed by the fifth working day in July.

	UK Limited	US Inc	Germany GmbH
	£	$	EUR
Amount owed by			
UK Limited	–	60,000	96,000
US Inc.	100,000	–	70,000
Germany GmbH	196,000	294,000	–
	296,000	354,000	166,000

The group's central treasury provides the following exchange rates to estimate netting payments: Euro 1 = £ 0.7 and £1 = $1.50.

The reference currency for multilateral netting is sterling.

Analysis
Outstanding debts and net payments are translated into sterling at the given exchange rates.

	UK Limited	US Inc	Germany GmbH
(Netting currency)	£	£	£
Owes	(107,200)	(149,000)	(392,000)
Is owed	296,000	236,000	116,200
Net amount receivable/ payable	188,800	87,000	(275,800)
		× 1.50	× 1/0.70
In local currency	£188,800	$130,500	Euro (394,000)

The company's bank will be asked to quote prices for the purchase of Euro 394,000 and the sale of $130,500. Rates quoted are: $1.52 = £1 and Euro 0.68 = £1.

The netting payments will be quickly recomputed at these rates.

	UK Limited	US Inc	Germany GmbH
	£	£	£
Owes	(104,754)	(147,600)	(389,421)
Is owed	296,000	232,895	112,880
Is owed/(owes) – net	191,246	85,295	(276,541)
		× 1.52	× 1/0.68
In local currency	GBP191,246	USD129,648	EUR(406,678)

The bank will be informed that the company wishes to sell Euro 406,678 and to buy $129,648, both in exchange for sterling. Instructions will be sent to Germany GmbH to pay Euro 406,678 to the bank, and to the bank to pay $129,648 into US Inc.'s bank account.

The netting company's central bank account will show the following transactions.

	£
Income from sale of Euro 406,678	276,541
Payment for purchase of $129,648	(85,295)
Payment to UK Limited	(191,246)
Net balance	0

The Netting Process

Netting imposes a payments discipline by enforcing a timetable for payments on regular settlement days. A possible timetable for cross-border netting is shown below.

Days	Action
Seven days before settlement	Companies within the netting scheme prepare details of the payments they are due to make, by currency. This information is sent by fax or electronically to the netting center or netting bank.
Four days before settlement	The netting center or bank confirms the net settlement obligations/net amounts due with the participating companies. On confirmation, transfer instructions are issued.
Two days before effect settlement	Foreign exchange is bought or sold (spot) to the payments. Transactions are arranged by the netting center or bank. Details of the currency transactions are sent to the participants concerned.
Settlement day	Settlement takes place two days later, on the value date for spot FX transactions.
Three days after settlement	Participants are provided with notification of the invoices that have been settled.

Advantages of Netting

Netting arrangements have several advantages, compared with systems that allow subsidiaries to arrange payments between themselves on mutually agreeable terms. While implementation of the Euro will greatly simplify netting arrangements in the Euro bloc, netting principles will continue to be used as many significant trading countries such as the UK, Brazil, Poland, Turkey, and Canada, will be trading partners.

Multilateral Netting Benefits

Netting is suitable only for companies that have a significant volume of trading exchanges.

The benefits of netting between companies in the same country are mainly qualitative rather than quantitative. It imposes discipline on the settlement of inter-company debts within a group. With fixed settlement dates, group companies are able to forecast their cash flows more accurately. Also there can be the advantage of simpler administration by reducing the number of inter-company payments for settling debts.

With cross-border multilateral netting, there can be quantitative as well as qualitative benefits, including

- a reduction in bank transfer charges, because there will be fewer cross-border payments
- a shorter cross-border float time that could be arranged with the netting bank
- fewer foreign exchange conversions
- possibly better foreign exchange conversion rates, for larger amounts of currency.

Netting systems must be administered. If a company has an in-house system, someone in the netting center or treasury department must select payment information, issue payment instructions and, where cross-border netting applies, arrange foreign exchange transactions.

Netting systems also can provide for leading and lagging payments, to control the liquidity of group companies. If one company within the group has cash surpluses, the netting center can instruct it to make lead payments, without taking the full period of credit normally allowed. Similarly, companies with a low cash balance or an overdraft might be permitted to lag payments beyond their due date.

Re-invoicing and Factoring

When multinationals establish a central treasury function for pooling and netting, they might also introduce a system of either re-invoicing or factoring. The purpose of re-invoicing or factoring is to improve the control of cash flows within the group. Currency exposures can be centralized, the settlement of payments managed more easily and liquidity within group companies more easily controlled, because leading and lagging payments can be directly controlled.

Re-invoicing Centers

Netting payments due to and from subsidiaries within a group can be arranged through a re-invoicing center. Netting is not the purpose for which a re-invoicing center is established, but it is a function that can be provided.

A re-invoicing center is set up as a subsidiary within a multinational group to help with cash management and foreign currency exposure management. The center often will be located in a country where tax benefits can be obtained, and where there are no exchange controls. A US multinational, for example, might have a re-invoicing center established as an offshore company in Belgium or the Netherlands.

A re-invoicing center is invoiced by subsidiaries in the group for

- cross-border transfers of goods and services by them to other subsidiaries, and
- exports to external (non-group) customers.

The center then produces another invoice for the subsidiary or external customer that is buying the goods or services.

Re-invoicing Center

INTRA-GROUP CROSS-BORDER TRANSFERS

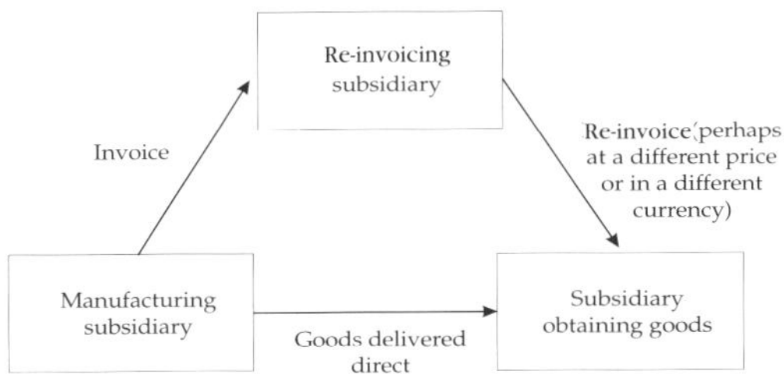

EXPORTS

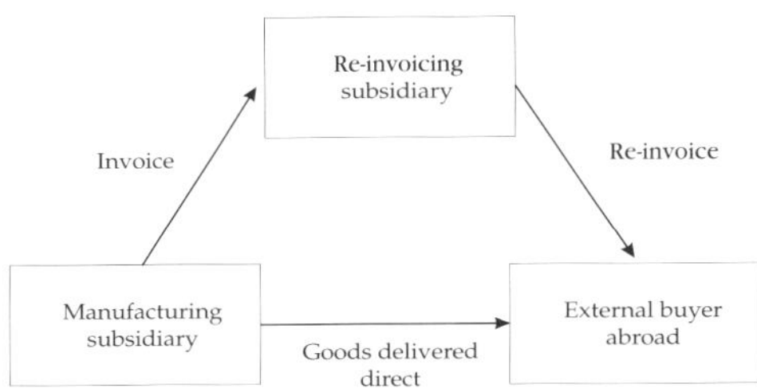

The re-invoicing center takes title to the goods or services provided even though it does not take physical possession of the goods or benefit from the services. It is sent an invoice and then sells the goods or services to the subsidiary that has received them.

By re-invoicing all cross-border sales by companies in the group, the center is able to organize foreign currency transactions centrally and on a large scale.

- Bank charges for foreign currency transactions are reduced.
- By dealing in larger quantities of currency, it should obtain better exchange rates from dealing banks.
- Foreign currency exposures can be reduced.
- Liquidity within the group can be managed efficiently.

The potential benefits of a re-invoicing company must justify the costs of establishing and operating the company and only large multinationals are likely to consider their potential.

Multicurrency Re-invoicing

With multicurrency re-invoicing, currency exposures can be centralized within the re-invoicing center. For example, suppose that a multinational has three subsidiaries, in France, the UK and Italy that sell to other group companies around the world. Using re-invoicing, purchasing subsidiaries can be invoiced in their domestic currency, Euro, or dollars, and the selling subsidiaries can be paid in domestic currency too. This is illustrated below.

Re-invoicing Center: Centralized Currency Exposures

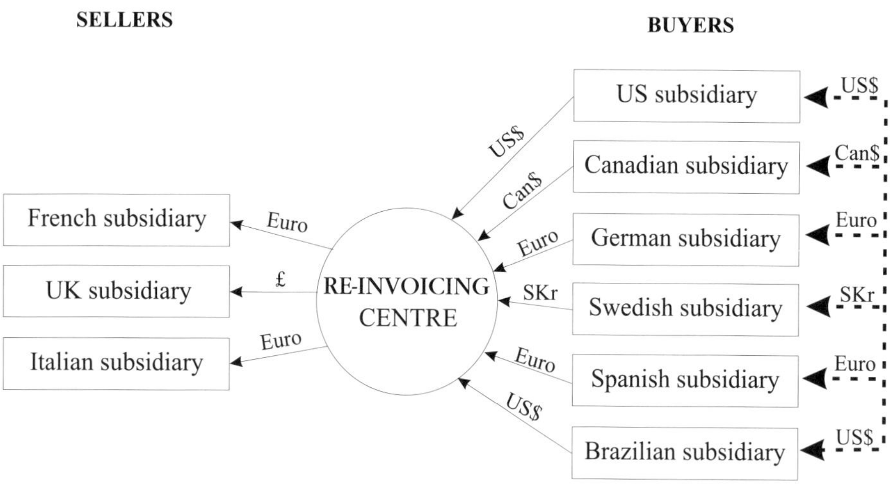

Factoring

An alternative to re-invoicing is factoring. The central treasury department handles invoices for goods and services between subsidiaries in the group, collects the payments and remits the payments to the seller.

Factoring

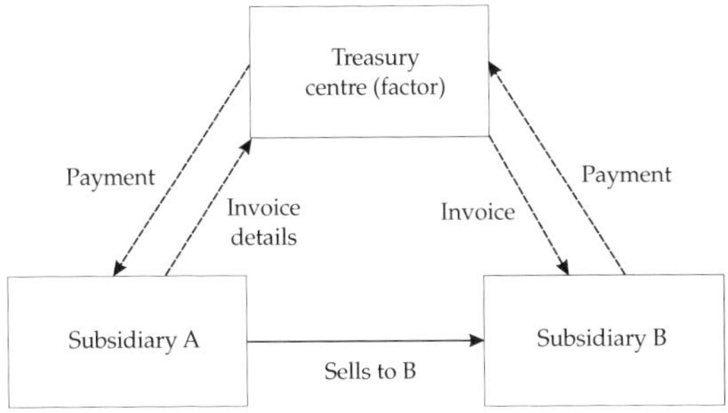

Liquidity Leveling

Liquidity leveling, as its name implies, is an arrangement for spreading liquidity around a group of companies by means of formalized short-term borrowing and lending arrangements. It relies on the regular issue of in-house instruments that are similar to commercial paper. Subsidiaries with a cash shortage issue these instruments (with a maturity of 30 days or 60 days, etc) and those with a cash surplus buy them if the rate offered is suitable. The group's in-house bank or central treasury can organize liquidity leveling.

Cash Pooling and Concentration Accounts

Companies with several bank accounts can arrange with their bank to combine the cash balances on each account, to minimize overdraft requirements or to optimize the use of surplus cash. Arrangements can take the form of either pooling or concentration accounts.

Pooling

A company with several bank accounts can use a cash pooling arrangement, typically one for each business unit. Under the arrangement any surplus funds are transferred from the business unit's account to a central account (the cash pool). If any business unit's account needs additional cash, there will be a transfer from the central cash pool.

- If the central cash pool is in surplus, these amalgamated funds can be invested.
- If the cash pool is in deficit, further borrowing will be arranged centrally.

Pooling arrangements between bank accounts in the same country make sense when significant cash balances and overdrafts are involved. Suppose for example that a company or group of companies has a surplus balance of $100,000 in one account and an overdraft of $100,000 in a second account. Without pooling, the $100,000 surplus would be invested at one rate of interest, and interest would be paid at a higher rate on the overdraft balance. Pooling will allow the surplus to offset the overdraft, thus saving the company the cost of the interest spread between the rate on deposits and the rate for overdrafts.

For a company with cash surpluses, pooling allows it to invest at a higher rate of interest because larger sums would be invested, and longer maturities are possible. Investing for longer maturities might not be an attractive option when the yield curve is inverse.

A central treasury also could be able to negotiate a better rate of interest than separate business units by borrowing in larger amounts, or by borrowing for periods that take advantage of the yield curve.

There are a number of factors involved in arranging a cash pooling system.

- The number of business units with a separate bank account.
- The number of different banks. Not all accounts need be with the same bank.
- The location of the bank accounts, particularly the country of location.
- The service the bank, or banks, is willing to offer to assist with the administration of a cash pooling arrangement, such as the automatic transfer of funds to or from the cash pool.

Example

A company has four subsidiaries, each with its own bank account. A pooling arrangement is operated by the group whereby cash balances in each account are swept up into a central account, and deficits on any account are wiped out by a transfer of cash from the central account.

The cash position of each account requires daily monitoring. Suppose, for example, that the cash balances towards the end of the day are as follows:

	Cash balance
	$
Subsidiary 1	+60,000
Subsidiary 2 (deficit)	–35,000
Subsidiary 3	+5,000
Subsidiary 4	+20,000
Head office central pooling account	+100,000

The cash surpluses of subsidiaries 1, 3 and 4 ($85,000) would be transferred to the central pooling account, and $35,000 would be paid from the central account to subsidiary 2's account, to eliminate its deficit. This would leave $150,000 in the central pool, some of which could then be invested or placed on deposit elsewhere, leaving an amount for contingency funds.

A pooling system could be arranged where the group's main business units each have a separate bank account for receiving income from customers and making only small payments. Larger payments, to most suppliers, for wages and salaries, tax payments, etc., would be made from the central pool account. Under this arrangement cash should always flow in to the cash pool from the other business unit bank accounts, and cash should never have to flow out to the business units. This would simplify administration of the cash pool.

Administration also would be simplified by arrangements with the company's bank for the automatic sweeping of surplus balances into the central pool, and the automatic elimination of deficits on individual accounts by means of transfers from the central pool. The bank would require specifications of the pooling arrangements, and would inform the company (daily, or at any other required frequency) of cash transfers and the balance on the central pool account.

Zero Balance Account

An alternative pooling arrangement is the zero balance account (ZBA).

Checks presented for payment that day against each business unit's bank account are totaled. Each account is then credited with exactly the amount of funds required to meet these payments, leaving the balance on the account at zero. These funds will be transferred automatically from the company's central cash pool account.

ZBAs are useful when a company wants to improve its cash monitoring by maintaining separate accounts for cash income and cash payments, for example, by having separate disbursement accounts for

- trade suppliers
- wages and salaries
- taxation
- miscellaneous items.

Each disbursement ZBA account will be funded whenever necessary to meet payments from the company's central cash account.

Example
Alpha operates with six separate bank accounts.

Account
1. central account, used for banking receipts from customers
2. payment account for salaries
3. payment account for trade suppliers
4. payment account for taxation
5. payment account for dividends
6. payment account for other expenditure items.

It has arranged with its bank that cash should be transferred each day from Account 1 to the other accounts, as necessary, to meet payments due from that account on that day. If salary payments of $800,000 were due on July 31, for example, this amount would be transferred from Account 1 to Account 2 on July 31 to meet the payment.

Target Balances

In some cases, a company might agree with its bank to maintain a minimum cash balance in each account, in return for negotiating lower bank charges for other services.

In most cases, a company will have a certain cash balance it wants to maintain in each account to meet credit commitments and contingencies. Cash pooling arrangements therefore will usually include an element of target balancing, with only funds in excess of the target balance transferred from each account to the central pool.

Bank Head Office Collection Account

A company could want to control its cash centrally, but receive cash at many different locations. An example is a nationwide retailing company. Each local shop or outlet will pay in cash and checks to its own local branch of the bank, and the funds would then be transferred to the head office's central account.

If the treasurer at head office wants to know at the beginning of the day how much will be received into the head office account during that day, the bank might be unable to provide the information, because it doesn't know how much will be transferred during the day for cash and checks paid in at other branches.

To overcome this problem, the company could use a collection account at the bank's head office. All money paid in by the shops or outlets to their local branch will be transferred to the bank head office collection account and automatically transferred to the company's central account, held with its own local branch. Information about receipts during the day then can be obtained from the bank's head office.

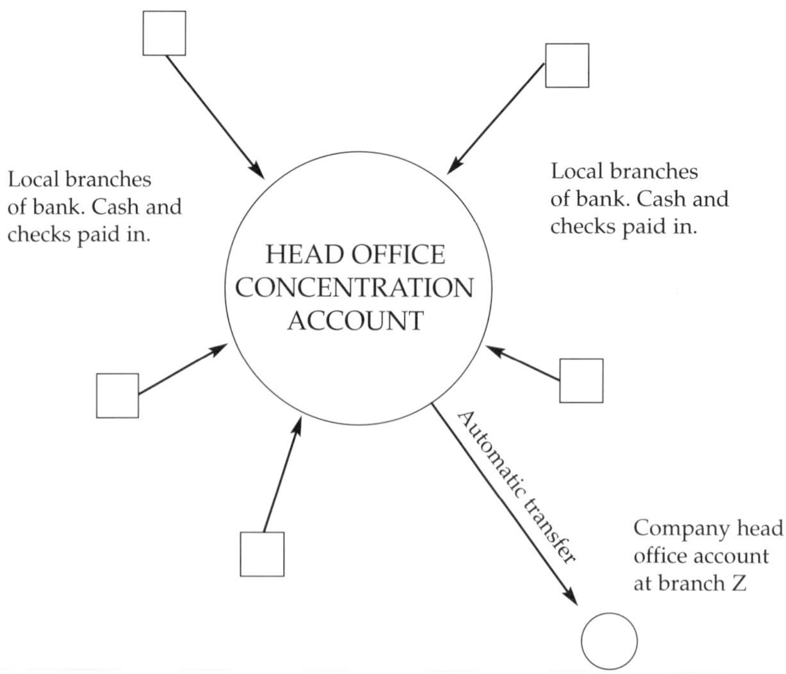

Daylight Exposures

A bank will expect a company's pooling and balancing arrangements to represent a square position on the account at the end of the banking day. The bank also will look at the intra-day or daylight exposure to which it is subject in operating the account. This is a function of timing mismatches in flows where a company, anticipating inward credits during the day, makes outward payments prior to the receipts arriving, thereby creating a debit position on the account for up to several hours. This isn't a problem provided that payment invariably arrives prior to the end of the banking day and the amounts involved are reasonable relative to the size of the company's normal banking volumes.

Problems do arise, however, if the daylight exposure is substantial or the expected inward flows do not arrive on the appointed day. In such circumstances the bank may insist on receipt prior to payment and deny the company investment access to funds received late in the day. The best practice in such instances is for a company to make arrangements with its bank for the funds to be invested in an interest-earning deposit account if the receipt is delayed beyond the effective close of the money markets and banking system.

Internal Overdrafts

When a system of cash pooling is in operation, local business units will not be allowed to arrange their own borrowing facilities. Cash deficits will be made good by transfers from the central cash pool, and any funding requirements for the group as a whole organized centrally.

As a measure to control cash management within the business units, head office might impose an internal overdraft limit on each unit. This is the maximum amount of cash that the central treasury will transfer to the unit to make up its cash deficit. The size of the overdraft limit should be agreed between head office and the business unit, and the ability of the unit to remain within its limit would be a performance measure by which unit management could be assessed.

- The internal overdraft limit could be varied during the course of each year, to allow for seasonal variations in the annual trading cycle of the business unit.
- The overdraft limit(s) should be reset regularly, probably as a part of the annual budgeting process.
- The limit should apply either to the daily overdraft limit (and overall limit) or the month-end overdraft position only.

Managers of business units would be expected to remain within their overdraft limit. Head office should not refuse to supply cash when a business unit needs to exceed its limit, because this could be damaging to the business. However, penalties of notional interest on excess overdraft balances might be charged to the business unit within the company's internal management accounting system, to draw attention to the unsatisfactory cash position of the business unit, and its cost to the group.

Taxation Aspects of Cash Pooling

There could be a tax problem with cash pooling when

- the holding company acts as the central banker, managing the cash pool, and
- the holding company does not carry out any trading activities, and is therefore an investment company (owning shares in the subsidiaries of the group).

Suppose that in such a situation, a subsidiary transfers surplus cash to the central cash pool, and the holding company rewards it by paying interest on the sum transferred. Because the interest would be paid by an investment company to a non-bank, the payment would not be an allowable expense for tax purposes for a UK-based company, whereas the interest income of the subsidiary would be taxable. Such an arrangement would be tax-inefficient.

This problem can be overcome, but should nevertheless be handled carefully. It might be decided that no interest is payable to subsidiaries on cash transferred to the cash pool. Alternatively in the UK, the Inland

Revenue might accept that the holding company has a trade of providing treasury services to its subsidiaries. If this argument is accepted, all interest on short-term borrowings paid by the holding company would be allowable for tax, including interest paid to subsidiaries, provided the interest cost is incurred wholly and exclusively for the purposes of carrying out its trade.

Cash pooling presents another tax problem when there are overseas subsidiaries in the group. The Inland Revenue might argue that the UK central treasury is acting as an agent on behalf of each foreign subsidiary, that therefore has a tax presence in the UK. To overcome this problem, the central treasury function could be based outside the UK (in an offshore company). In practice it is unusual for tax reasons for a UK-based treasury department to manage a cash pool for its foreign subsidiaries.

Cross-Border Pooling

Cross-border pooling is a more complex arrangement. There are several potential difficulties:

- transfer charges
- clearance delay
- currency risk
- tax implications.

Implementation of the Euro is expected to simplify greatly cross-border arrangements for intra-EU pooling that form the bulk of transfers for EU companies. However, significant amounts of extra-EU trade and pooling are expected to continue although they will represent a smaller portion of total transfers.

The higher bank charges and longer clearance delay for cross-border funds transfers can mean that the cost of transferring funds to a central pool account exceeds the benefits, particularly for smaller amounts or for short durations. Pooling arrangements might therefore restrict transfers of funds to cash surpluses above a certain value and with a minimum expected duration.

Currency risk would occur if the transferred funds were converted into a second currency. Adverse movements in the exchange rate between the currencies could leave the company facing an exchange loss.

The tax implications of cross-border funds transfers would have to be considered. The funds would move from one tax jurisdiction to another and interest could be taxed at a different rate. There also could be withholding taxes on the transfer.

In spite of the difficulties, some multinationals have opted for cross-border pooling because the benefits outweigh the costs.

When a cross-border pooling arrangement is used, the multinational might set up an offshore in-house central bank, for example in Bermuda. The bank would receive cash surpluses above a given size from other group companies and relend to those in need of funds. If the offshore company were a profit center, it would relend at a higher rate than it pays on pooled deposits, but at a rate below or competitive with lending rates of external banks.

Concentration Accounts (Offset Arrangements)

Concentration accounts (offset arrangements) are a form of cash pooling, but without the need to transfer cash from one account to another.

With a concentration account-banking configuration, all the company's bank accounts must be with the same bank. At a simple level, this will involve several different accounts with the same branch. At the most complex level, it will involve accounts in several different currencies and in different countries.

All the bank accounts of the company are consolidated, and the balances on all the accounts taken as a single total for the purpose of interest calculations. Cleared credit balances are offset against cleared debit balances, and interest paid only on the net balances. This arrangement saves the need for daily transfers of cash between accounts, bookkeeping for these transfers as well as bank charges for the transfers. In these respects a concentration account system is simpler than cash pooling.

For example, suppose that a company has four bank accounts with XYZ Bank, and the balances on these accounts are:

Account 1	\$30,000 credit
Account 2	\$20,000 credit
Account 3	\$40,000 debit (overdrawn)
Account 4	\$5,000 debit (overdrawn).

If a concentration account arrangement were operated, the company would have a net credit balance of \$5,000 and would not pay overdraft interest.

All major banks in many countries offer this service for accounts in the domestic currency. More complex accounts in several countries and in several currencies will have to be negotiated with the bank.

Concentration accounts and offset arrangements are used both by individual companies that operate several bank accounts and by groups where two or more companies in the group have accounts with the same bank. This can cause problems if one company in the group goes bankrupt because the bank does not automatically have the legal right to obtain cash from the accounts of the other companies. The solution for a group of companies therefore would be to have a cash-pooling arrangement in which all surplus funds are brought into the same account or else have appropriate legal documentation drafted to clarify this matter.

Banking Configurations and Investing Surplus Cash

Whether a company has just one bank account or several, it should have a system for using surplus cash by investing it as quickly as possible and for so long as possible.

A small company with sufficient surplus cash might simply arrange with its bank to open a money market deposit account, and invest its funds at money market rates. These accounts are available for funds in excess of a minimum amount of perhaps $10,000.

Banks will, for a fee, offer more sophisticated systems for investing surplus cash, including cash pools or concentration account arrangements. These systems include

- automatic investment
- zero balancing
- full set-off.

With *automatic investment*, the bank automatically will invest overnight the total of cleared balances on the company's current accounts at the end of each day. Automatic investment can be arranged where the company has just one account with its bank. It also can be arranged for more complex banking configurations, for example a cash pool. The arrangement can be unattractive, however, in terms of interest rates received, and frequently the cut-off time is too early to sweep up credits received late in the day.

With *zero balancing*, the bank automatically will transfer the cleared balance on each of the company's accounts into a single account, leaving the balance on these accounts at zero. This central balance (cash pool balance) is reported to the customer, and can be invested at the highest rate obtainable, probably at the customer's own initiative.

A *full set-off* system is operated within a concentration account type of configuration. The balance on each bank account is left intact, but the forecast net credit position of the bank accounts in total is reported as being available for investment. Any cash investment would draw on the company's central account, to bring the net balance on all the accounts to zero.

Example 1
A company has six accounts, with the following balances:

Account	Balance	
1	$35,000	debit (overdrawn)
2	$20,000	credit
3	$50,000	credit
4	$40,000	credit
5	$10,000	debit (overdrawn)
Central account	$15,000	debit (overdrawn)
Total	$50,000	credit

The net $50,000 would be available for investment (perhaps automatic investment) out of the central account. This would bring the net balance on all six accounts to zero, and on the central account to $60,000 debit. The company would not be charged overdraft interest on any account, because overdrafts on some accounts are offset by surplus cash balances on others.

There is some confusion in banking terms, and *full set-off* might be termed *zero balancing* by some bankers and treasurers.

A company should select a system negotiated with a bank for investing surplus cash from its accounts and whose benefits are likely to justify the time and effort needed to operate it. It is likely to be more profitable to run the risk of over-investing and occasionally having an overdraft than to leave an uninvested current account surplus earning no interest. Decisions about investing forecast surpluses should not be over-cautious, and result in investing less cash than the total surplus available.

Example 2
Beta has a pooling arrangement whereby cleared balances from 15 bank accounts within the group are swept into a central account. Management is now considering two options for the overnight investment of cleared funds in the central account.

Option 1
To invest cleared funds overnight at 0.03% per day. The amount invested would be the forecast cleared balance for the day. This forecast is produced at 11am each day. If the actual cleared balance is less than the forecast, the company would invest more cash than it has available, and its central account would go into deficit as a consequence. Overdraft interest would cost 0.04% per day.

Option 2
To maintain a minimum amount of $50,000 in the central pool, earning no interest. The estimated cleared funds for the day minus this $50,000 would be invested overnight at 0.03% per day.

To assist with its evaluation, Beta's management has looked at its daily estimates of cleared funds during the previous week, and the actual cleared funds in the central pool account as at the end of each day.

	Forecast cleared balance	**Actual cleared balance**
	$	**$**
Day 1	1,000,000	990,000
Day 2	1,000,000	1,050,000
Day 3	1,200,000	1,200,000
Day 4	1,500,000	1,450,000
Day 5	1,100,000	1,150,000

Analysis
If the company selected Option 1, and forecast and actual cleared balances for five days were as in the table, its net income for the week would have been as follows:

Policy Option 1

	Forecast cleared balance	Actual cleared balance	Income for the day	Overdraft charge
	$	$	$	$
Day 1	1,000,000	990,000	300	(4)
Day 2	1,000,000	1,050,000	300	
Day 3	1,200,000	1,200,000	360	
Day 4	1,500,000	1,450,000	450	(20)
Day 5	1,100,000	1,150,000	330	
			1,740	(24)
			1,716	

With Option 2, investing the forecast balance, minus the $50,000 in the central pool, the income for the week would have been as follows:

Policy Option 2

	Forecast cleared funds	Amount invested overnight	Interest earned
	$	$	$
Day 1	1,000,000	950,000	285
Day 2	1,000,000	950,000	285
Day 3	1,200,000	1,150,000	345
Day 4	1,500,000	1,450,000	435
Day 5	1,100,000	1,050,000	315
			1,665

In spite of occasional overdraft costs these sample figures suggest that Option 1 is likely to be more profitable.

Bank Accounts Overseas

It should not be assumed that cash held in a bank account abroad could be readily transferred to a central account. There are three reasons why this might not be the case.

First, overseas business units could be reluctant to remit funds to a head office in a different country. This is a problem of local self-interest.

Second, the subsidiary might prefer to hold on to its cash to meet its own possible future requirements, and resist head-office requirements to transfer cash, especially temporary surpluses. A company might be unable to arrange a banking configuration that provides for a convenient transfer of funds. As a result there could be delays in arranging transfers.

Third, local laws and regulations could thwart efficient banking arrangements. A well-publicized example in 1990 was the large amount of cash reportedly held by Polly Peck in northern Cyprus, at a time when the rest of the group had a damaging shortage of cash. Contrary to expectation, the cash apparently available in northern Cyprus could not or would not be transferred back to the UK when it was needed.

Summary

The most efficient cash management system for a company will depend on the nature of the company's cash flows. For a large multinational, for example, the most suitable arrangements might be for an offshore subsidiary to be responsible for managing cash balances, organizing cross-border and multi-currency pooling, and netting payments between subsidiaries in the group. There might be a central cash pool for each currency, with each of these central accounts located in a different country, and with an electronic banking system installed to allow head office to manage the pooling cash flows.

The key questions, inevitably, are what benefits could be derived from an alternative system, in terms of interest cost savings or lower bank charges, and how much extra would it cost to switch to this system.

Locating a central treasury for cross-border pooling, netting and re-invoicing or factoring will depend on several key factors:

- taxation
- availability of skilled staff

- access to financial markets. (The chosen site should be in a country that has ready access to financial markets, for investing cash, FX transactions, etc.)
- geographical closeness to group operations. This is desirable because the treasury department would avoid being isolated from the operating divisions of the group.

The chosen site must be able to avoid large withholding taxes on cross-border interest payments. Other tax incentives in a particular country might be significant.

9

Electronic Banking Systems

Automated systems for cash management vary in purpose and design. Some are developed in-house, and others are electronic banking systems supplied to customers by their bank. They are typically PC-based although interfaces to the main accounting ledgers on a mainframe may be implemented.

In-House Automated Cash Management Systems

Systems can be developed in-house to improve the speed and flexibility of cash management. Cash forecasts for example are commonly based on a computer model. An online payments system can be used that could provide a direct link to the company's ledgers. Requests for checks or payments by bank transfer could be input from a remote terminal to a central computer. Each request would be validated to ensure that an authorized person had originated it and that the payment details were in order. Payment then would be authorized online by the appropriate manager, and a check printed automatically, or a bank transfer instruction cleared for sending.

EBS

An electronic banking system (EBS) allows a company to log-on to computerized information and the payments systems of its bank from a

PC or dumb terminal in its own office. Banks market off-the-shelf, proprietary systems to medium-sized companies, as well as to large companies. Features vary from bank to bank, and the types of service on offer can be tailored to the needs and size of the company.

Electronic banking systems mainly provide the following:

- Balance reporting and transactions reporting
- Funds transfers
- Decision support services.

Main Elements of Electronic Banking Systems

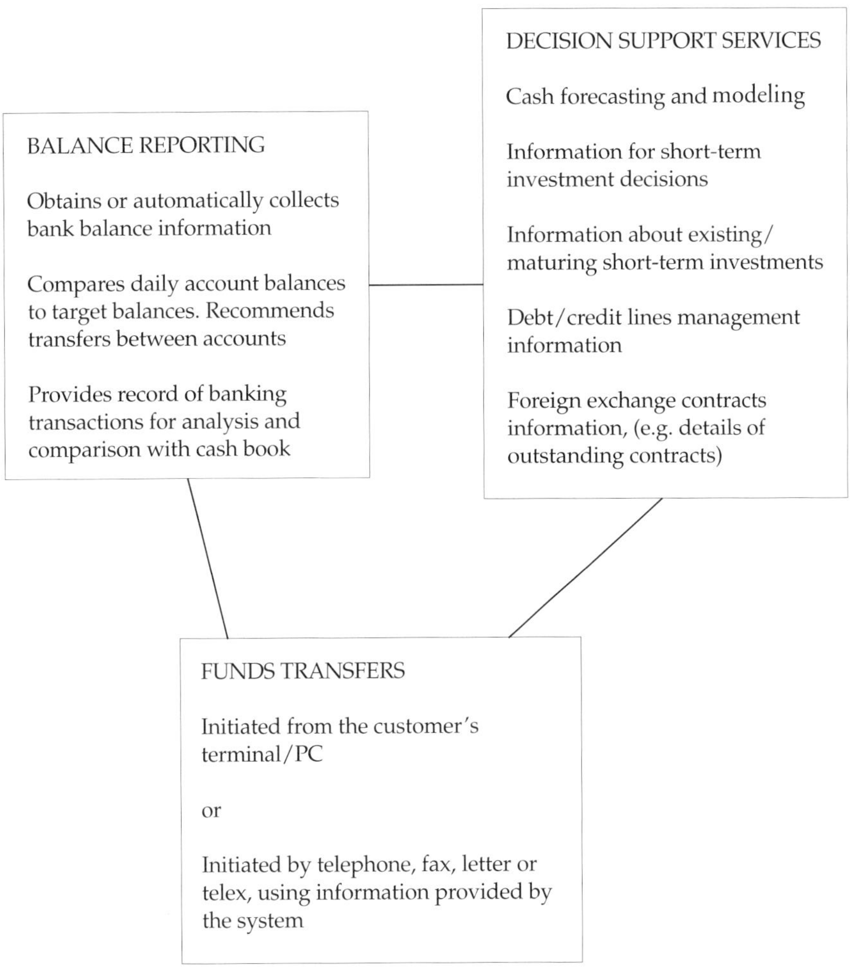

Balance Reporting and Transactions Reporting

An electronic banking system provides information about cash balances and banking transactions that have gone through an account.

Balance information can be reported in three ways.

- The night's closing position. This shows the cleared balances on each account as at the end of the previous day.
- The next morning's opening position. This adjusts last night's closing position for items that will clear through the account that day, such as checks, standing orders, direct debits and BACS items.
- Intra-day real time position. This updates the cleared balance during the day as credits and debits are attributed to the account.

A financial controller or treasurer can use this information to prepare an estimate of the company's closing cash position for the current day. The morning's opening position can be adjusted for the same-day value transfers that should be made into or from each account – CHAPS items and other intra-bank transfers, such as money payments from abroad.

An EBS also can provide transaction information for the current day, the previous day and if required, further back in time. This is detailed information about receipts and payment transactions going through the account. Balances on short-term investment accounts also are provided, typically indicating the rate of interest being paid on those accounts.

On some systems, balance and transaction information is provided for bank accounts abroad, held by subsidiaries or branches of international companies. This enables a company's head office to monitor its overseas accounts.

A system can give a company access to information about its accounts with that bank only, not with accounts at any other bank. For large companies, information provided by one or more banks could be fed into the company's own automated cash-management system, and merged with internally generated information.

In the US that traditionally has been subject to interstate banking restrictions (although these barriers have been gradually disappearing because of market pressures), corporations will use a number of different banks, and electronic banking systems must therefore provide account and balance information from a number of different banks within a single information system.

Funds Transfers and Other Transactions

Electronic banking systems can be used to initiate a number of banking transactions, such as

- funds transfers
- money-market investment transactions
- foreign-exchange transactions.

Payment instructions to a bank can be initiated electronically and international payments carried out using SWIFT messaging.

With the rapid growth of the internet, there has been much interest in developing secure payment systems using data encryption. Simple purchases of goods already can be made using this technology. Such internet payment systems for use by corporates would operate independently of banks but much remains to be done and full implementation is still a way off.

Automated payments systems, either as stand-alone systems or as part of a larger EBS, continue to be developed. Users can have the option, for example, of pre-setting value dates for paperless transfers, and for giving instructions for next-day and same-day payments.

Systems should enable the company to provide authorized confirmation to the bank for any transaction it has initiated, for example by producing an automatically written confirmation of any transaction.

Decision Support Services

There are several decision support services that electronic banking systems can provide to assist corporate cash management. They include:

- Balance history reporting. This is simply a list of daily balances on an account that can be checked to identify any continued idle balances. A decision then could be taken to transfer or invest funds if idle balances exist.
- Cash forecasting and target balance projections. Information from electronic banking systems can be used to assist with cash forecasting based on a computer model. Cash forecasts can be established as target balances for the subsequent monitoring and control of cash flows and balances. Only some of the information needed for forecasting can be fed in from an EBS, the rest must be provided from other sources or by the company itself.
- Netting cash flows. Systems can be used to assist with the netting of cash flows between accounts, and the reduction of banking transaction costs.
- Market information. Information is provided about current exchange rates and interest rates.

Administrative Support Features

Electronic banking systems normally will include a number of administrative support features that help with the management of a company's bank accounts. They include a facility to

- order statements, check books and paying-in books
- transmit messages to the branch holding the company's account
- order the transfer of funds between the company's own accounts with the bank.

Some systems incorporate treasury accounting facilities and the ability to download either processed data or raw data into the main corporate accounting system.

Multibank and Multinational Reporting

A potential weakness of some electronic banking systems is that the information they provide is restricted to account balances and transactions with just one bank. Such systems are still dominated by bank proprietary systems and the absence of common standards and record formats creates operating difficulties in pulling together information from various banks.

Many companies (particularly very large businesses) have accounts with two or more banks, often in different countries. Unless information can be obtained from the different banks and integrated into a single reporting system, electronic banking systems will be of limited use because the integration of information from different banking sources would have to be done manually, or by a separate computer program.

There are electronic banking systems available, however, for companies requiring multibank and multinational/multicurrency reporting.

The use of electronic banking systems for reporting cross-border cash balances is expected to increase substantially over the next few years. Most banks are prepared to participate in multibank balance reporting, whereby they feed customer balance information, directly or indirectly, into the systems of other banks, at the customer's request. A difficulty with multibank reporting systems, however, is the lack of standardization of formats amongst the banks. Reports from one bank might not be easily assimilated into another bank's balance reporting system. Multibank reporting services/software therefore have been developed to take output from different banks and reformat the information.

The more cumbersome alternative to multibank reporting systems is to have an electronic banking system for each bank with which the company has an account.

In most cases such a multibank reporting system is provided by a third-party network, and banks agree to download account information on to the network via a bureau. For example, suppose that a company has accounts with five banks in four different countries. It will ask all the banks to supply account information to the network via their bureau. This information will be transmitted to the bureau for the company's main bank, for transmission to the customer. All the bureaus with links to the network have software than can consolidate the account data from several banks into a standard screen format.

Third party networks are popular with banks because they avoid the need for one bank to send account information about a customer directly to another bank. In this way they maintain confidentiality and prevent the customer's main bank from gaining access to information that could give it a competitive edge over the company's other banks.

Systems that use third party networks generally are more complex and more costly than banks' own systems that are linked up to the database of just one bank.

Not all multibank systems are provided through a third party network. Some banks have their own international system. The customer asks its other banks to provide account information to the main bank that consolidates the information for transmission to the customer. One bank consolidation systems have not been popular because of the reluctance of other banks to provide confidential information to the main bank.

Equipment

An EBS user needs a PC/terminal and modem. To access the system, the user either telephones the network/system number, providing a password to gain entry, or establishes an electronic link-up. To access its own account information within the system, the company will have to give one or more additional passwords.

Information will be displayed on the user's screen, and also can be printed out, or copied on to the company's own computer files (currently for larger systems only).

Security

Security issues are paramount. Banks are fully aware of the need for secure balance reporting and funds transfer systems, given the sophistication of computer hackers who are intent on committing damage or fraud. Consequently they have developed and continue to evolve, measures to protect the integrity of information and physical cash.

EBS systems incorporate a multiple password or pass code structure that grants different levels of authority and/or access to different people within the company. Some systems employ encryption devices at the terminals of both the EBS customer and the bank to encode information prior to transmission and decode it on arrival. This ensures that it is unintelligible to hackers who could intercept it en route to the bank's terminal. Some systems incorporate the value, the currency and/or the destination bank details in the encryption code combining it in logarithmic form to ensure that any illegal rerouting will be aborted automatically at the bank's terminal. Others issue authorized personnel with a small device that generates a confidential algorithm and updates the alphanumeric password every two minutes. When logging onto the system the device generates a password in conjunction with the user's password. Such real-time update systems provide strong security.

Some terminals have limited physical access, by being located in a secure area, a keyboard lock or an entry code for the terminal.

Treasury Workstations

Cash management and other elements of treasury management are closely interrelated.

Treasury workstations are computer based cash management systems sold by banks. They provide information for decisionmaking to the manager, combined with a facility for initiating transactions. Workstation functions include balance reporting, monitoring positions on foreign exchange contracts and letters of credit, debt and investment monitoring and payments initiation.

A treasury workstation can be described as a treasurer's personal computer that combines in-house data with data provided electronically by the company's bank(s). The data is then processed using either software developed by the company, for example a cash flow model or foreign exchange exposure model, and/or off-the-shelf software packages. The software typically will include a spreadsheet-modeling package.

Data provided to the workstation from the company's in-house sources will include budget data, foreign exchange positions and the current position of trading and other transactions such as outstanding creditors and debtors, payment terms, etc.

Data provided electronically from the bank(s) will include balance information, lending information, and market data such as exchange rates and interest rates, although this data can also be fed into the workstation from other data providers.

A treasury workstation provides a decision support system that can be used to process data for different aspects of cash management.

- Forecasting cash and setting target balances and also for what if cash flow modeling.
- Pre-deal support. Before approaching any bank to negotiate a foreign exchange or borrowing transaction, checks can be made on the company's outstanding position and credit lines with the bank.
- Information about currency exposures. Current market information on exchange rates can be used to mark-to-market the company's foreign currency position.
- Producing management reports on cash forecasts, foreign exchange exposures, hedging positions taken, etc.

Electronic Data Interchange (EDI)

EDI provides communications between two organizations (customer and supplier) without manual intervention at any stage in the communications process. Originating in the US, EDI has rapidly extended into the rest of the world and depends on the sending and receiving parties agreeing a common structure and format for electronic messages.

Additional security can be provided by exchanging software keys enabling data encryption technology such as PGP (Pretty Good Privacy) to be used, thereby rendering the electronic communications absolutely illegible and impervious to cracking. Current 128-bit encryption technology means that a PC attempting to crack the PGP code would have to work full time on the problem for over three months – more than enough time to compensate for a one-week validity in replacing keys.

EDI promises considerable improvement in electronic banking services, particularly for automated payments, but it remains to be seen what EDI services banks develop in view of emerging protocols.

Costs

The cost of an electronic banking system depends on its size and sophistication. If a medium-sized company uses an EBS provided directly by its bank, it will probably pay the bank

- an installation fee to link up to the system, and/or the purchase cost of a software package for the system, and
- a monthly charge.

Telephone charges for dial-up links probably will be at local rates payable to the telephone line supplier. For continuous data links, the company will, of course, have to pay a line rental charge.

For a larger system provided via a third party network, the network operator will levy charges that the bank will pass on to its customers.

Advantages and Disadvantages

The advantages of an EBS arise from its speed and the availability of information. A company should be able to use an EBS to control its cash payments by delaying instructions to transfer funds until the last moment. Readily accessible information about cash balances also should help companies use cash more effectively, transferring funds between accounts or investing short-term surpluses.

The potential advantages of electronic banking are

- better decisionmaking and control over cash
- fewer errors and oversights
- faster reconciliations, reconciling bank-account information with internal accounting records
- smaller staff requirements and lower costs.

An EBS costs money that the benefits from the system will have to justify. For companies with occasional and fairly predictable cash flows, balance information and information about the current day's transactions can be obtained from the bank by telephone fairly early each day. This often will be a cheaper way of getting all the information required. An EBS would be unnecessary in such cases.

Although the cost of electronic banking systems can be considerable, their use is now widespread, even among smaller companies.

Summary

Electronic banking systems have developed to fill an information gap for companies in their cash management. Although banks can give customers information about their cash position on request, it is the customer's responsibility to ask for it. Information can be overlooked. It might be easy, for example, for a cash manager to forget about a maturing investment and funds being transferred back into a current account, simply by overlooking a diary reminder. Electronic banking systems can reduce the probability that such information will go unnoticed and that appropriate actions might not be taken.

The more sophisticated electronic banking systems now provide facilities that overlap with sophisticated treasury management systems, such as

- Dealer support capability, monitoring currency and interest-rate exposure positions and quantifying the extent of and the need for corrective action;
- Credit-exposure reporting, monitoring the extent of the company's exposure to each counterparty bank for total banking business (and comparing this exposure with internal credit limits that the company has set itself for that bank);
- Cash diaries, giving advance notice of forthcoming cash flows;
- Cash-forecasting systems, providing standard layouts for use in the cash-forecasting process and an interface with the balance reporting part of the system.

Conclusion

All companies, regardless of their size, need to manage cash in order to maintain liquidity. If a company needs to borrow, the aim of its cash-management policy should be to keep interest costs as low as possible. In contrast, a company with surplus funds to invest has the aim of maximizing interest income.

This book has focused on three important aspects of cash management:

- cash collection/payment
- banking configurations
- electronic banking systems.

Companies should actively pursue the best methods for collecting and depositing their receipts. They also should ensure that cash payments are made, surplus cash is invested and funding requirements are met.

Whether the cash-management function is the responsibility of a centralized treasury or a local business unit, existing practices should be reviewed regularly to ensure that cash is being handled effectively and efficiently. The development of computer models for cash forecasting, and electronic banking systems for transferring funds, has greatly enhanced the cash-management function. Continued investment in such systems is vital to enhance the speed, accuracy, and security of management-information systems. Greater efficiency and better control of cash should help management achieve their aims of higher interest income or lower interest costs.

Glossary

Bilateral Netting
Netting arrangement between two parties.

Cash Book
An account in the ledger of a business. It is used to record cash receipts and cash payments.

CHAPS
Clearing House Automated Payments System. A system for making automated same-day value payments.

Check and Credit Clearing Company Limited
Organization responsible for clearing high-volume, paper-based payments such as checks and Bank Giro transfers. Managed by APACS.

CHIPS
Clearinghouse Interbank Payments System. A US system for sending dollar payment instructions electronically to give same-day value to the recipient. Used primarily for international payments.

Clearance Delay
Float time within the banking system for clearing a payment and giving the payee good value (cleared funds) in his account.

Clearing
The process by which banks exchange checks and other payments between their customers, and settle for the net difference owed by or from each bank to the others. The payer then has funds taken from his account and the payee receives cleared funds.

Clearing House
Center/organization where clearing takes place and clearing-house members arrange to settle payments between themselves.

Concentration Account
See Offset Arrangement.

Configuration
A bank account configuration is a system by which a company organizes its banking arrangements for cash handling.

Confirmed Letter of Credit
A letter of credit that is guaranteed (confirmed) by a second bank, often in the exporter's country. See Letter of Credit.

Correspondent Bank
A bank in one country that will perform a variety of services on behalf of another bank and its customers in a second country. Correspondent bank services include collecting payments from abroad. Correspondent banks maintain an account for each other, for settlement of payments.

Daylight Exposure
The amount of payments from an account during a day, in anticipation of receipts of funds later in the day to leave a zero balance on the account at the end of the day. There is an exposure to the risk that the anticipated receipts might not occur.

Direct Debit
Instruction sent by a beneficiary to the bank of the payer, authorized by the payer, to make regular payments from the payer's account. The beneficiary can amend the amount of direct debit payments, until such time as the payer cancels the direct-debit instruction (mandate).

Documentary Credit
See Letter of Credit.

EFT
Electronic funds transfer. Computerized payment instructions sent from a terminal.

Electronic Data Interchange (EDI)
A system for the electronic transmission of information between two organizations, without any manual intervention. Equipment speaks to equipment.

Factoring
Arrangement by which a financial center within a group collects payments on behalf of subsidiaries for goods/services sold to external buyers or to other subsidiaries.

FedWire
Government-owned system for same-day funds transfers between banks.

Float
Amount of cash received, but whereby value for which (cleared funds) has not yet been received in a bank account.

Float Time
The time between receiving a payment and obtaining good value (cleared funds) in a bank account.

Lagging
Payment later than due date.

Leading
Payment ahead of due date.

Letter of Credit
Method of payment in international trade. A bank, acting on the instructions of a customer (an importer), guarantees payment to a third party (an exporter), by accepting a paying bill of exchange, against provision by the exporter of specified documentation in accordance with specified terms and conditions of the letter of credit.

Lockbox
System for collecting payments used in the US, although considered outdated. A bank receives payments on behalf of a lockbox customer and arranges to clear them.

Lodgment Delay
Float time from receiving a payment to presenting it to a bank (lodging it with a bank) for paying into a bank account.

Multilateral Netting
Netting arrangement between more than two parties, involving a netting payment to or from each party by a netting center or netting bank.

Netting
An arrangement (within a group of companies) for payments between the bank accounts of subsidiaries that trade regularly with each other. Payments receivable from or payable to all other subsidiaries are netted into a single amount. This is paid to or received from a netting center (a central treasury department or a netting bank). Netting occurs at predetermined and regular intervals, perhaps monthly.

Netting Center or Netting Bank
Administrative center for netting arrangements and payments.

Nostro Account
An account held by a bank with a correspondent bank abroad, in the domestic currency of the corespondent bank.

Offset Arrangement
A form of cash pooling without the need for transferring funds to a central pool. The balances on each account in the scheme are added together. Credit balances on some accounts offset debit balances on others. Also called a concentration account arrangement.

Pooling
Arrangement for a company with several bank accounts whereby surplus funds are transferred from each account into a central pool. If any account has an overdraft (debit) balance, this is cleared by a transfer from the central pool.

Pre-payment Cards
A form of electronic payment using a card which is pre-loaded (credited) with cash value and can be used to buy an increasing range of goods and services. Phone cards are an early example of the pre-payment card concept, also known as an electronic purse.

Purchase Cards
Charge cards that provide businesses with a way of making trade payments. They have the potential for cost savings over current, paper-based, processes.

Re-invoicing Center
Financial center within a group that is invoiced for goods/services sold by subsidiaries to external buyers or to other subsidiaries. The center then issues its own invoice to the buyer. A re-invoicing center is able to administer foreign exchange exposures and netting arrangements within the group.

Relationship Banking
A relationship with one bank (perhaps two or three) whereby the customer channels all or most of its banking business through that bank.

Same-Day Clearing
Clearing a payment on the day that it is initiated. The payee receives cleared funds on that day.

Standing Order
Instruction by a payer to his bank to make regular fixed payments to the account of a specified beneficiary.

SWIFT
Society for Worldwide Interbank Financial Telecommunications. An organization of banks, linked by a communications network that is used for sending international money transfer instructions.

Target Balance
Minimum cash balance that individual bank accounts in a pooling arrangement are permitted to retain. Only balances in excess of this minimum are transferred to the cash pool.

Telegraphic Transfer (TT)
A cable payment order. A method of payment by bank transfer. Still in use, although declining.

Town Clearing
System based on a limited number of Town Clearing banks in the City of London, for same-day value check clearing. Checks must be for payments above £500,000.

Transaction Banking
Obtaining banking services from any of several banks, choosing the bank offering the cheapest cost, best dealing rate or specialization in that service.

Transmission Delay
Float time from a payer sending a payment, to its receipt by the payee. Usually associated with delivery time for the payment through the post.

Treasury Workstation
A computer-based cash management system supplied by a bank, that allows the user to combine information from in-house sources with information provided by the bank. It can be described as a treasurer's personal computer, or a computerized decision-support system for cash management.

Value
Cleared funds (available in a bank account for immediate use).

Value-Dated Payment
A payment for which the payer specifies the date on which the payment is to be made and the recipient obtain good value for the funds. BACS payments and SWIFT payments are value-dated.

Vostro Account
An account held with a bank in its domestic currency, by a correspondent bank in another country. For example, a US bank might have a correspondent bank in Switzerland. This Swiss bank would maintain a dollar account with the US bank. To the US bank, this would be a vostro account.

Withholding Tax
A tax on interest or dividend payments. The payment is made net of tax and the tax withheld is paid to the authorities.

Yield Curve
A term used to describe how current interest rates vary according to the term-to-maturity of the loan or deposit. When longer-term interest rates are higher than shorter-term rates, the yield curve is upward sloping or normal. When longer-term interest rates are lower than shorter-term rates, the yield curve is inverse. These interest rate comparisons can be shown on a graph; hence the term yield curve.

Zero-Balance Account

Arrangement in which a company uses several bank accounts for making payments. Sufficient funds are provided to each account each day from a central pool, to make payments due from the account. This leaves each payments account with a zero balance, and all surplus funds are concentrated in the cash pool.

Index